PHRASEBOOK
- BULGARIAN -

THE MOST IMPORTANT PHRASES

This phrasebook contains
the most important
phrases and questions
for basic communication
Everything you need
to survive overseas

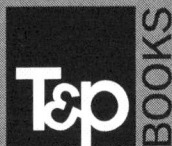

By Andrey Taranov

T&P BOOKS

Phrasebook + 1500-word dictionary

English-Bulgarian phrasebook & concise dictionary

By Andrey Taranov

The collection of "Everything Will Be Okay" travel phrasebooks published by T&P Books is designed for people traveling abroad for tourism and business. The phrasebooks contain what matters most - the essentials for basic communication. This is an indispensable set of phrases to "survive" while abroad.

Another section of the book also provides a small dictionary with more than 1,500 useful words arranged alphabetically. The dictionary includes a lot of gastronomic terms and will be helpful when ordering food at a restaurant or buying groceries at the store.

T&P Books Publishing
www.tpbooks.com

ISBN: 978-1-78492-444-7

This book is also available in E-book formats.
Please visit www.tpbooks.com or the major online bookstores.

FOREWORD

The collection of "Everything Will Be Okay" travel phrasebooks published by T&P Books is designed for people traveling abroad for tourism and business. The phrasebooks contain what matters most - the essentials for basic communication. This is an indispensable set of phrases to "survive" while abroad.

This phrasebook will help you in most cases where you need to ask something, get directions, find out how much something costs, etc. It can also resolve difficult communication situations where gestures just won't help.

This book contains a lot of phrases that have been grouped according to the most relevant topics. A separate section of the book also provides a small dictionary with more than 1,500 important and useful words.

Take "Everything Will Be Okay" phrasebook with you on the road and you'll have an irreplaceable traveling companion who will help you find your way out of any situation and teach you to not fear speaking with foreigners.

TABLE OF CONTENTS

T&P Books Publishing

PRONUNCIATION

Letter	Bulgarian example	T&P phonetic alphabet	English example
А а	кантар	[a]	shorter than in ask
Б б	бор	[b]	baby, book
В в	водач	[v]	very, river
Г г	година	[g]	game, gold
Д д	данък	[d]	day, doctor
Е е	елен	[ɛ]	man, bad
Ж ж	живот	[ʒ]	forge, pleasure
З з	зеле	[z]	zebra, please
И и	ивица	[i]	shorter than in feet
Й й	йод	[j]	yes, New York
К к	колиба	[k]	clock, kiss
Л л	локва	[l]	lace, people
М м	майка	[m]	magic, milk
Н н	намаление	[n]	name, normal
О о	одеяло	[o], [ɔ]	drop, baught
П п	пари	[p]	pencil, private
Р р	речник	[r]	rice, radio
С с	секира	[s]	city, boss
Т т	торба	[t]	tourist, trip
У у	утре	[u]	book
Ф ф	филия	[f]	face, food
Х х	храна	[h], [x]	as in Scots loch
Ц ц	царевица	[ts]	cats, tsetse fly
Ч ч	чанта	[tʃ]	church, French
Ш ш	шал	[ʃ]	machine, shark
Щ щ	щъркел	[ʃ]	machine, shark
Ъ ъ	огън	[ɪ]	big, America
Ь ь	миньор	[ʲ]	soft sign - no sound
нь	треньор	[ɲ]	canyon, new
ль	бельо	[ʎ]	daily, million
ть	фотьойл	[t]	tune, student
Ю ю	ютия	[ju]	youth, usually
Я я	яхния	[jɑ]	young, yard

LIST OF ABBREVIATIONS

English abbreviations

ab.	-	about
adj	-	adjective
adv	-	adverb
anim.	-	animate
as adj	-	attributive noun used as adjective
e.g.	-	for example
etc.	-	et cetera
fam.	-	familiar
fem.	-	feminine
form.	-	formal
inanim.	-	inanimate
masc.	-	masculine
math	-	mathematics
mil.	-	military
n	-	noun
pl	-	plural
pron.	-	pronoun
sb	-	somebody
sing.	-	singular
sth	-	something
v aux	-	auxiliary verb
vi	-	intransitive verb
vi, vt	-	intransitive, transitive verb
vt	-	transitive verb

Bulgarian abbreviations

ж	-	feminine noun
ж мн	-	feminine plural
м	-	masculine noun
м мн	-	masculine plural
м, ж	-	masculine, feminine
мн	-	plural
с	-	neuter
с мн	-	neuter plural

T&P BOOKS

BULGARIAN PHRASEBOOK

This section contains
important phrases that may
come in handy in various
real-life situations.
The phrasebook will help
you ask for directions, clarify
a price, buy tickets, and
order food at a restaurant

T&P Books Publishing

PHRASEBOOK CONTENTS

T&P Books Publishing

The bare minimum

Excuse me, ...	**Извинете, ...** [izvi'nɛtɛ, ...]
Hello.	**Здравейте.** [zdra'vɛjtɛ]
Thank you.	**Благодаря.** [blagɔda'rʲa]
Good bye.	**Довиждане.** [dɔ'viʒdanɛ]
Yes.	**Да.** [da]
No.	**Не.** [nɛ]
I don't know.	**Аз не знам.** [az nɛ znam]
Where? | Where to? | When?	**Къде? | Накъде? | Кога?** [kə'dɛ? | nakə'dɛ? | kɔ'ga?]

I need ...	**Трябва ми ...** ['trʲabva mi ...]
I want ...	**Аз искам ...** [az 'iskam ...]
Do you have ...?	**Имате ли ...?** ['imatɛ li ...?]
Is there a ... here?	**Тук има ли ...?** [tuk 'ima li ...?]
May I ...?	**Мога ли ...?** ['mɔga li ...?]
..., please (polite request)	**Моля.** ['mɔʎa]

I'm looking for ...	**Аз търся ...** [az 'tərsʲa ...]
restroom	**тоалетна** [tɔa'letna]
ATM	**банкомат** [bankɔ'mat]
pharmacy (drugstore)	**аптека** [ap'tɛka]
hospital	**болница** ['bɔlnitsa]
police station	**полицейски участък** [pɔli'tsɛjski u'tʃastək]
subway	**метро** [mɛt'rɔ]

taxi	**такси** ['taksi]
train station	**гара** ['gara]

My name is …	**Казвам се …** ['kazvam sɛ …]
What's your name?	**Как се казвате?** [kak sɛ 'kazvatɛ?]
Could you please help me?	**Помогнете ми, моля.** [pɔmɔg'nɛtɛ mi, 'mɔʎa]
I've got a problem.	**Аз имам проблем.** [az 'imam prɔb'lem]
I don't feel well.	**Лошо ми е.** ['lɔʃɔ mi ɛ]
Call an ambulance!	**Повикайте бърза помощ!** [pɔvi'kajtɛ 'bərza 'pɔmɔʃt!]
May I make a call?	**Може ли да се обадя?** ['mɔʒɛ li da sɛ ɔ'badʲa?]

I'm sorry.	**Извинявам се.** [izvi'ɲavam sɛ]
You're welcome.	**Моля.** ['mɔʎa]

I, me	**аз** [az]
you (inform.)	**ти** [ti]
he	**той** [tɔj]
she	**тя** [tʲa]
they (masc.)	**те** [tɛ]
they (fem.)	**те** [tɛ]
we	**ние** ['niɛ]
you (pl)	**вие** ['viɛ]
you (sg, form.)	**Вие** ['viɛ]

ENTRANCE	**ВХОД** [vhɔd]
EXIT	**ИЗХОД** ['izhɔd]
OUT OF ORDER	**НЕ РАБОТИ** [nɛ 'rabɔti]
CLOSED	**ЗАТВОРЕНО** [zat'vɔrɛnɔ]

OPEN	**ОТВОРЕНО**
	[ɔt'vɔrɛnɔ]
FOR WOMEN	**ЗА ЖЕНИ**
	[za ʒɛ'ni]
FOR MEN	**ЗА МЪЖЕ**
	[za mə'ʒɛ]

Questions

Where?	**Къде?** [kə'dɛ?]
Where to?	**Накъде?** [nakə'dɛ?]
Where from?	**Откъде?** [ɔtkə'dɛ?]
Why?	**Защо?** [za'ʃtɔ?]
For what reason?	**По каква причина?** [pɔ kak'va pri'tʃina?]
When?	**Кога?** [kɔ'ga?]

How long?	**За колко?** [za 'kɔlkɔ?]
At what time?	**В колко?** [v 'kɔlkɔ?]
How much?	**Колко струва?** ['kɔlkɔ 'struva?]
Do you have ...?	**Имате ли ...?** ['imatɛ li ...?]
Where is ...?	**Къде се намира ...?** [kə'dɛ sɛ na'mira ...?]

What time is it?	**Колко е часът?** ['kɔlkɔ ɛ tʃa'sət?]
May I make a call?	**Може ли да се обадя?** ['mɔʒɛ li da sɛ ɔ'badʲa?]
Who's there?	**Кой е там?** [kɔj ɛ tam?]
Can I smoke here?	**Мога ли тук да пуша?** ['mɔga li tuk da 'puʃa?]
May I ...?	**Мога ли ...?** ['mɔga li ...?]

Needs

I'd like …	**Аз бих искал /искала/ …** [az bih 'iskal /'iskala/ …]
I don't want …	**Аз не искам …** [az nɛ 'iskam …]
I'm thirsty.	**Аз искам да пия.** [az 'iskam da pi'ja]
I want to sleep.	**Аз искам да спя.** [az 'iskam da spʲa]
I want …	**Аз искам …** [az 'iskam …]
to wash up	**да се измия** [da sɛ izmi'ja]
to brush my teeth	**да си мия зъбите** [da si 'miʲa zə'bitɛ]
to rest a while	**малко да си почина** ['malkɔ da si pɔ'ʧina]
to change my clothes	**да се преоблека** [da sɛ prɛɔble'ka]
to go back to the hotel	**да се върна в хотела** [da sɛ 'vərna v hɔ'tɛla]
to buy …	**да купя …** [da 'kupʲa …]
to go to …	**да отида …** [da ɔ'tida …]
to visit …	**да посетя …** [da pɔsɛ'tʲa …]
to meet with …	**да се срещна с …** [da sɛ 'srɛʃtna s …]
to make a call	**да се обадя** [da sɛ ɔ'badʲa]
I'm tired.	**Аз се изморих.** [az sɛ izmɔ'rih]
We are tired.	**Ние се изморихме.** ['niɛ sɛ izmɔ'rihmɛ]
I'm cold.	**Студено ми е.** [stu'dɛnɔ mi ɛ]
I'm hot.	**Топло ми е.** [t'ɔplɔ mi ɛ]
I'm OK.	**Нормално ми е.** [nɔr'malnɔ mi ɛ]

I need to make a call.

Трябва да се обадя.
['trʲabva da sɛ ɔ'badʲa]

I need to go to the restroom.

Искам да отида в тоалетната.
['iskam da ɔ'tida v tɔa'letnata]

I have to go.

Трябва да тръгвам.
['trʲabva da 'trəgvam]

I have to go now.

Сега трябва да тръгвам.
[sɛ'ga 'trʲabva da 'trəgvam]

Asking for directions

Excuse me, ...	**Извинете, ...** [izvi'nɛtɛ, ...]
Where is ...?	**Къде се намира ...?** [kə'dɛ sɛ na'mira ...?]
Which way is ...?	**В коя посока се намира ...?** [v kɔ'a pɔ'sɔka sɛ na'mira ...?]
Could you help me, please?	**Помогнете ми, моля.** [pɔmɔg'nɛtɛ mi, 'mɔʎa]
I'm looking for ...	**Аз търся ...** [az 'tərsʲa ...]
I'm looking for the exit.	**Аз търся изход.** [az 'tərsʲa 'izhɔd]
I'm going to ...	**Аз пътувам до ...** [az pə'tuvam dɔ ...]
Am I going the right way to ...?	**Правилно ли вървя ...?** ['pravilnɔ li vər'vʲa ...?]
Is it far?	**Далече ли е?** [da'lɛtʃɛ li ɛ?]
Can I get there on foot?	**Ще стигна ли дотам пеша?** [ʃtɛ 'stigna li dɔ'tam 'pɛʃa?]
Can you show me on the map?	**Покажете ми на картата, моля.** [pɔka'ʒɛtɛ mi na 'kartata, 'mɔʎa]
Show me where we are right now.	**Покажете, къде сме сега.** [pɔka'ʒɛtɛ, kə'dɛ smɛ sɛ'ga]
Here	**Тук** [tuk]
There	**Там** [tam]
This way	**Тука** ['tuka]
Turn right.	**Завийте надясно.** [za'vijtɛ na'dʲasnɔ]
Turn left.	**Завийте наляво.** [za'vijtɛ na'ʎavɔ]
first (second, third) turn	**първи (втори, трети) завой** ['pərvi ('vtɔri, 'trɛti) za'vɔj]
to the right	**надясно** [na'dʲasnɔ]

to the left

наляво
[na'ʎavɔ]

Go straight.

Вървете направо.
[vər'vɛtɛ nap'ravɔ]

Signs

WELCOME!	**ДОБРЕ ДОШЛИ!**
	[dɔb'rɛ dɔ'ʃli!]
ENTRANCE	**ВХОД**
	[vhɔd]
EXIT	**ИЗХОД**
	['izhɔd]
PUSH	**БУТНИ**
	[but'ni]
PULL	**ДРЪПНИ**
	[drəp'ni]
OPEN	**ОТВОРЕНО**
	[ɔt'vɔrɛnɔ]
CLOSED	**ЗАТВОРЕНО**
	[zat'vɔrɛnɔ]
FOR WOMEN	**ЗА ЖЕНИ**
	[za ʒɛ'ni]
FOR MEN	**ЗА МЪЖЕ**
	[za mə'ʒɛ]
MEN, GENTS	**МЪЖКА ТОАЛЕТНА**
	['məʒka tɔa'letna]
WOMEN, LADIES	**ЖЕНСКА ТОАЛЕТНА**
	['ʒɛnska tɔa'letna]
DISCOUNTS	**НАМАЛЕНИЯ**
	[nama'lenia]
SALE	**РАЗПРОДАЖБА**
	[razprɔ'daʒba]
FREE	**БЕЗПЛАТНО**
	[bɛz'platnɔ]
NEW!	**НОВИНА!**
	[nɔvi'na!]
ATTENTION!	**ВНИМАНИЕ!**
	[vni'maniɛ!]
NO VACANCIES	**НЯМА МЕСТА**
	['ɲama mɛs'ta]
RESERVED	**РЕЗЕРВИРАНО**
	[rɛzɛr'viranɔ]
ADMINISTRATION	**АДМИНИСТРАЦИЯ**
	[administ'racia]
STAFF ONLY	**САМО ЗА ПЕРСОНАЛА**
	['samɔ za pɛrsɔ'nala]

BEWARE OF THE DOG! **ЛОШО КУЧЕ**
[ˈlɔʃɔ kutʃɛ]

NO SMOKING! **НЕ СЕ ПУШИ!**
[nɛ sɛ ˈpuʃi!]

DO NOT TOUCH! **НЕ ПИПАЙ С РЪЦЕТЕ!**
[nɛ piˈpaj s rəˈcɛtɛ!]

DANGEROUS **ОПАСНО**
[ɔˈpasnɔ]

DANGER **ОПАСНОСТ**
[ɔˈpasnɔst]

HIGH VOLTAGE **ВИСОКО НАПРЕЖЕНИЕ**
[viˈsɔkɔ naprɛˈʒɛniɛ]

NO SWIMMING! **КЪПАНЕТО Е ЗАБРАНЕНО**
[ˈkəpanɛtɔ ɛ zabraˈnɛnɔ]

OUT OF ORDER **НЕ РАБОТИ**
[nɛ ˈrabɔti]

FLAMMABLE **ОГНЕОПАСНО**
[ɔgnɛɔˈpasnɔ]

FORBIDDEN **ЗАБРАНЕНО**
[zabraˈnɛnɔ]

NO TRESPASSING! **ПРЕМИНАВАНЕТО Е ЗАБРАНЕНО**
[prɛmiˈnavanɛtɔ ɛ zabraˈnɛnɔ]

WET PAINT **БОЯДИСАНО**
[bɔˈaˈdisanɔ]

CLOSED FOR RENOVATIONS **ЗАТВОРЕНО ЗА РЕМОНТ**
[zatˈvɔrɛnɔ za rɛˈmɔnt]

WORKS AHEAD **РЕМОНТНИ РАБОТИ**
[rɛˈmɔntni ˈrabɔti]

DETOUR **ЗАОБИКАЛЯНЕ**
[zaɔbiˈkaʎanɛ]

Transportation. General phrases

plane	**самолет**
	[samɔ'let]
train	**влак**
	[vlak]
bus	**автобус**
	[avtɔ'bus]
ferry	**фериборт**
	['fɛribɔt]
taxi	**такси**
	['taksi]
car	**кола**
	['kɔla]

schedule	**разписание**
	[razpi'saniɛ]
Where can I see the schedule?	**Къде мога да видя разписанието?**
	[kə'dɛ 'mɔga da 'vidʲa razpi'saniɛtɔ?]
workdays (weekdays)	**работни дни**
	[ra'bɔtni dni]
weekends	**почивни дни**
	[pɔ'tʃivni dni]
holidays	**празнични дни**
	['praznitʃni dni]

DEPARTURE	**ЗАМИНАВАНЕ**
	[zami'navanɛ]
ARRIVAL	**ПРИСТИГАНЕ**
	[pri'stiganɛ]
DELAYED	**ЗАКЪСНЯВА**
	[zakəs'ɲava]
CANCELED	**ОТМЕНЕН**
	[ɔtmɛ'nɛn]

next (train, etc.)	**следващ**
	['sledvaʃt]
first	**първи**
	['pərvi]
last	**последен**
	[pɔs'ledɛn]

When is the next ...?	**Кога е следващият ...?**
	[kɔ'ga ɛ 'sledvaʃtiʲat ...?]
When is the first ...?	**Кога тръгва първият ...?**
	[kɔ'ga 'trəgva 'pərviʲat ...?]

When is the last ...?

Кога тръгва последният ...?
[kɔ'ga 'trəgva 'pɔsledniʲat ...?]

transfer (change of trains, etc.)

прекачване
[prɛ'katʃvanɛ]

to make a transfer

да правя прекачване
[da 'pravʲa prɛ'katʃvanɛ]

Do I need to make a transfer?

Трябва ли да правя прекачване?
['trʲabva li da 'pravʲa prɛ'katʃvanɛ?]

Buying tickets

Where can I buy tickets?	**Къде мога да купя билети?** [kə'dɛ 'mɔga da 'kupʲa bi'leti?]
ticket	**билет** [bi'let]
to buy a ticket	**да купя билет** [da 'kupʲa bi'let]
ticket price	**цена на билета** [cɛ'na na bi'leta]
Where to?	**Накъде?** [nakə'dɛ?]
To what station?	**До коя станция?** [dɔ kɔ'ja 'stanciʲa?]
I need …	**Трябва ми …** ['trʲabva mi …]
one ticket	**един билет** [ɛ'din bi'let]
two tickets	**два билета** [dva bi'leta]
three tickets	**три билета** [tri bi'leta]
one-way	**в една посока** [v ɛd'na pɔ'sɔka]
round-trip	**отиване и връщане** [ɔ'tivanɛ i 'vrəʃtanɛ]
first class	**първа класа** ['pərva 'klasa]
second class	**втора класа** ['vtɔra 'klasa]
today	**днес** [dnɛs]
tomorrow	**утре** ['utrɛ]
the day after tomorrow	**вдругиден** ['vdrugidɛn]
in the morning	**сутринта** [sut'rinta]
in the afternoon	**през деня** [prɛz dɛ'ɲa]
in the evening	**вечерта** [vɛtʃɛr'ta]

aisle seat

място до коридора
['mʲastɔ dɔ kɔri'dɔra]

window seat

място до прозореца
['mʲastɔ dɔ prɔ'zɔrɛca]

How much?

Колко?
['kɔlkɔ?]

Can I pay by credit card?

Мога ли да платя с карта?
['mɔga li da pla'tʲa s 'karta?]

Bus

bus	**автобус** [avtɔ'bus]
intercity bus	**междуградски автобус** [mɛʒdu'gradski avtɔ'bus]
bus stop	**автобусна спирка** [avtɔ'busna 'spirka]
Where's the nearest bus stop?	**Къде се намира най-близката автобусна спирка?** [kə'dɛ sɛ na'mira naj-'blizkata avtɔ'busna 'spirka?]

number (bus ~, etc.)	**номер** ['nɔmɛr]
Which bus do I take to get to …?	**Кой номер автобус отива до …?** [kɔj 'nɔmɛr avtɔ'bus ɔ'tiva dɔ …?]
Does this bus go to …?	**Този автобус отива ли до …?** ['tɔzi avtɔ'bus ɔ'tiva li dɔ …?]
How frequent are the buses?	**Кога има автобуси?** [kɔ'ga 'ima avtɔ'busi?]

every 15 minutes	**на всеки 15 минути** [na 'vsɛki pɛt'nadɛsɛt mi'nuti]
every half hour	**на всеки половин час** [na 'vsɛki pɔlɔ'vin ʧas]
every hour	**на всеки час** [na 'vsɛki ʧas]
several times a day	**няколко пъти на ден** ['ɲakɔlkɔ 'pəti na dɛn]
… times a day	**… пъти на ден** [… 'pəti na dɛn]

schedule	**разписание** [razpi'saniɛ]
Where can I see the schedule?	**Къде мога да видя разписанието?** [kə'dɛ 'mɔga da 'vidʲa razpi'saniɛtɔ?]

When is the next bus?	**Кога е следващият автобус?** [kɔ'ga ɛ 'slɛdvaʃtiʲat avtɔ'bus?]
When is the first bus?	**Кога тръгва първият автобус?** [kɔ'ga trəgva 'pərviʲat avtɔ'bus?]
When is the last bus?	**Кога заминава последният автобус?** [kɔ'ga zami'nava pɔs'lɛdniʲat avtɔ'bus?]
stop	**спирка** ['spirka]

next stop

следваща спирка
['sledvaʃta 'spirka]

last stop (terminus)

последна спирка
[pɔs'ledna 'spirka]

Stop here, please.

Спрете тук, моля.
['sprɛtɛ tuk, 'mɔʎa]

Excuse me, this is my stop.

Може ли, това е моята спирка.
['mɔʒɛ li, tɔ'va ɛ 'mɔʲata 'spirka]

Train

train	**влак** [vlak]
suburban train	**крайградски влак** [kraj'gradski vlak]
long-distance train	**влак за далечни разстояния** [vlak za da'letʃni razstɔ'janiʲa]
train station	**гара** ['gara]
Excuse me, where is the exit to the platform?	**Извинявайте, къде е изхода към влаковете?** [izvi'ɲavajtɛ, kə'dɛ ɛ 'izhɔda kəm 'vlakɔvɛtɛ?]

Does this train go to ...?	**Този влак отива ли до ...?** ['tɔzi vlak ɔ'tiva li dɔ ...?]
next train	**следващ влак** ['sledvaʃt vlak]
When is the next train?	**Кога е следващият влак?** [kɔ'ga ɛ 'sledvaʃtiʲat vlak?]
Where can I see the schedule?	**Къде мога да видя разписанието?** [kə'dɛ 'mɔga da 'vidʲa razpi'saniɛtɔ?]
From which platform?	**От кой перон?** [ɔt kɔj pɛ'rɔn?]
When does the train arrive in ...?	**Кога влакът пристига в ...?** [kɔ'ga 'vlakət pris'tiga v ...?]

Please help me.	**Помогнете ми, моля.** [pɔmɔg'nɛtɛ mi, 'mɔʎa]
I'm looking for my seat.	**Аз търся мястото си.** [az 'tərsʲa 'mʲastɔtɔ si]
We're looking for our seats.	**Ние търсим местата си.** ['niɛ 'tərsim mɛs'tata si]

My seat is taken.	**Мястото ми е заето.** ['mʲastɔtɔ mi ɛ za'ɛtɔ]
Our seats are taken.	**Местата ни са заети.** [mɛs'tata ni sa za'ɛti]
I'm sorry but this is my seat.	**Извинявайте, но това е моето място.** [izvi'ɲavajtɛ, nɔ tɔ'va ɛ 'mɔɛtɔ 'mʲastɔ]

Is this seat taken?

Това място свободно ли е?
[tɔ'va 'mʲastɔ svɔ'bɔdnɔ li ɛ?]

May I sit here?

Мога ли да седна тук?
['mɔga li da 'sɛdna tuk?]

On the train. Dialogue (No ticket)

Ticket, please.
Билета ви, моля.
[bi'leta vi, 'mɔʎa]

I don't have a ticket.
Аз нямам билет.
[az 'ɲamam bi'let]

I lost my ticket.
Аз загубих билета си.
[az za'gubih bi'leta si]

I forgot my ticket at home.
Аз забравих билета си в къщи.
[az za'bravih bi'leta si v 'kəʃti]

You can buy a ticket from me.
Вие можете да си купите билет от мен.
['viɛ 'mɔʒɛtɛ da si 'kupitɛ bi'let ɔt mɛn]

You will also have to pay a fine.
Също така ще трябва да заплатите глоба.
['səʃtɔ ta'ka ʃtɛ 'trʲabva da za'platitɛ 'glɔba]

Okay.
Добре.
[dɔb'rɛ]

Where are you going?
Накъде пътувате?
[nakə'dɛ pə'tuvatɛ?]

I'm going to …
Аз пътувам до …
[az pə'tuvam dɔ …]

How much? I don't understand.
Колко? Не разбирам.
['kɔlkɔ? nɛ raz'biram]

Write it down, please.
Напишете, моля.
[napi'ʃɛtɛ, 'mɔʎa]

Okay. Can I pay with a credit card?
Добре. Мога ли да платя с карта?
[dɔb'rɛ. 'mɔga li da pla'tʲa s 'karta?]

Yes, you can.
Да. Можете.
[da. 'mɔʒɛtɛ]

Here's your receipt.
Заповядайте, вашата квитанция.
[zapɔ'vʲadajtɛ, vaʃata kvi'tancʲa]

Sorry about the fine.
Съжалявам за глобата.
[səʒa'ʎavam za 'glɔbata]

That's okay. It was my fault.
Няма нищо. Вината е моя.
['ɲama 'niʃtɔ. vi'nata ɛ 'mɔʲa]

Enjoy your trip.
Приятно пътуване.
[pri'jatnɔ pə'tuvanɛ]

Taxi

taxi	**такси** ['taksi]
taxi driver	**таксист** ['taksist]
to catch a taxi	**да взема такси** [da 'vzɛma 'taksi]
taxi stand	**стоянка на такси** [stɔ'janka na 'taksi]
Where can I get a taxi?	**Къде мога да взема такси?** [kə'dɛ 'mɔga da 'vzɛma 'taksi?]
to call a taxi	**да повикам такси** [da pɔ'vikam 'taksi]
I need a taxi.	**Трябва ми такси.** ['trʲabva mi 'taksi]
Right now.	**Точно сега.** ['tɔʧnɔ sɛ'ga]
What is your address (location)?	**Вашият адрес?** ['vaʃʲat ad'rɛs?]
My address is …	**Моят адрес е …** ['mɔʲat ad'rɛs ɛ …]
Your destination?	**Къде отивате?** [kə'dɛ ɔ'tivatɛ?]
Excuse me, …	**Извинете, …** [izvi'nɛtɛ, …]
Are you available?	**Свободни ли сте?** [svɔ'bɔdni li stɛ?]
How much is it to get to …?	**Каква е цената до …?** [kak'va ɛ cɛ'nata dɔ …?]
Do you know where it is?	**Знаете ли, къде е това?** ['znaɛtɛ li, kə'dɛ ɛ tɔ'va?]
Airport, please.	**До аерогарата, моля.** [dɔ aɛrɔ'garata, 'mɔʎa]
Stop here, please.	**Спрете тук, моля.** ['sprɛtɛ tuk, 'mɔʎa]
It's not here.	**Това не е тук.** [tɔ'va nɛ ɛ tuk]
This is the wrong address.	**Това е неправилен адрес.** [tɔ'va ɛ nɛ'pravilen ad'rɛs]
Turn left.	**наляво** [na'ʎavɔ]
Turn right.	**надясно** [na'dʲasnɔ]

How much do I owe you?

Колко ви дължа?
['kɔlkɔ vi dəl'ʒa?]

I'd like a receipt, please.

Дайте ми касов бон, моля.
['dajtɛ mi 'kasɔv bɔn, 'mɔʎa]

Keep the change.

Задръжте рестото.
[zad'rəʒtɛ 'rɛstɔtɔ]

Would you please wait for me?

Изчакайте ме, моля.
[iz'ʧakajtɛ mɛ, 'mɔʎa]

five minutes

пет минути
[pɛt mi'nuti]

ten minutes

десет минути
['dɛsɛt mi'nuti]

fifteen minutes

петнадесет минути
[pɛt'nadɛsɛt mi'nuti]

twenty minutes

двадесет минути
['dvadɛsɛt mi'nuti]

half an hour

половин час
[pɔ'lɔvin ʧas]

Hotel

Hello.
Здравейте.
[zdra'vɛjtɛ]

My name is …
Казвам се …
['kazvam sɛ …]

I have a reservation.
Аз резервирах стая.
[az rɛzɛr'virah 'staʲa]

I need …
Трябва ми …
['trʲabva mi …]

a single room
единична стая
[ɛdi'nitʃna 'staʲa]

a double room
двойна стая
['dvɔjna 'staʲa]

How much is that?
Колко струва?
['kɔlkɔ 'struva?]

That's a bit expensive.
Това е малко скъпо.
[tɔ'va ɛ 'malkɔ 'skəpɔ]

Do you have any other options?
Имате ли още нещо?
['imatɛ li 'ɔʃtɛ 'nɛʃtɔ?]

I'll take it.
Ще го взема.
[ʃtɛ gɔ 'vzɛma]

I'll pay in cash.
Ще платя в брой.
[ʃtɛ 'platʲa v brɔj]

I've got a problem.
Аз имам проблем.
[az 'imam prɔb'lem]

My … is broken.
Моят /моята/ … е счупен /счупена/.
['mɔʲat /'mɔʲata/ … ɛ 'stʃupɛn /'stʃupɛna/]

My … is out of order.
Моят /моята/ … не работи
['mɔʲat /'mɔʲata/ … nɛ 'rabɔti]

TV
моят телевизор
['mɔʲat tɛle'vizɔr]

air conditioning
моят климатик
['mɔʲat 'klimatik]

tap
моят кран
['mɔʲat kran]

shower
моят душ
['mɔʲat duʃ]

sink
моята мивка
['mɔʲata 'mivka]

safe
моят сейф
['mɔʲat sɛjf]

door lock	**моята ключалка** ['mɔ^jata klju'tʃalka]
electrical outlet	**моят контакт** ['mɔ^jat kɔn'takt]
hairdryer	**моят сешоар** ['mɔ^jat sɛʃɔ'ar]

I don't have ...	**Нямам ...** ['ɲamam ...]
water	**вода** [vɔ'da]
light	**ток** [tɔk]
electricity	**електричество** [ɛlek'tritʃɛstvɔ]

Can you give me ...?	**Може ли да ми дадете ...?** ['mɔʒɛ li da mi da'dɛtɛ ...?]
a towel	**хавлия** [hav'li^ja]
a blanket	**одеяло** [ɔdɛ'jalɔ]
slippers	**чехли** ['tʃɛhli]
a robe	**халат** [ha'lat]
shampoo	**шампоан** [ʃampɔ'an]
soap	**сапун** [sa'pun]

I'd like to change rooms.	**Бих искал /искала/ да сменя стаята си.** [bih 'iskal /'iskala/ da smɛ'ɲa 'sta^jata si]
I can't find my key.	**Не мога да намеря ключа си.** [nɛ 'mɔga da na'mɛr^ja 'kljutʃa si]
Could you open my room, please?	**Отворете моята стая, моля.** [ɔt'vɔrɛtɛ 'mɔ^jata 'sta^ja, 'mɔʎa]
Who's there?	**Кой е?** [kɔj ɛ?]
Come in!	**Влезте!** ['vlɛztɛ!]
Just a minute!	**Една минута!** [ɛd'na mi'nuta!]

Not right now, please.	**Моля, не сега.** ['mɔʎa, nɛ sɛ'ga]
Come to my room, please.	**Влезте при мен, моля.** ['vlɛztɛ pri mɛn, 'mɔʎa]

I'd like to order food service.	**Бих искал /искала/ да поръчам храна за стаята.** [bih 'iskal /'iskala/ da 'pɔrətʃam hra'na za 'staˌata]
My room number is …	**Номерът на стаята ми е ….** ['nɔmɛrət na 'staˌata mi ɛ ….]
I'm leaving …	**Заминавам …** [zami'navam …]
We're leaving …	**Ние заминаваме …** ['niɛ zami'navamɛ …]
right now	**сега** [sɛ'ga]
this afternoon	**днес след обяд** [dnɛs slɛd ɔ'bˌad]
tonight	**днес вечерта** [dnɛs vɛtʃɛr'ta]
tomorrow	**утре** ['utrɛ]
tomorrow morning	**утре сутринта** ['utrɛ sut'rinta]
tomorrow evening	**утре вечер** ['utrɛ 'vɛtʃɛr]
the day after tomorrow	**вдругиден** ['vdrugidɛn]

I'd like to pay.	**Бих искал /искала/ да заплатя.** [bih 'iskal /'iskala/ da zapla'tˌa]
Everything was wonderful.	**Всичко беше отлично.** [vsitʃkɔ 'bɛʃɛ ɔt'litʃnɔ]
Where can I get a taxi?	**Къде мога да взема такси?** [kə'dɛ 'mɔga da 'vzɛma 'taksi?]
Would you call a taxi for me, please?	**Повикайте ми такси, моля.** [pɔvi'kajtɛ mi 'taksi, 'mɔʎa]

Restaurant

Can I look at the menu, please?	**Мога ли да видя менюто ви?** ['mɔga li da 'vidʲa mɛ'njutɔ vi?]
Table for one.	**Маса за един човек.** ['masa za ɛ'din ʧɔ'vɛk]
There are two (three, four) of us.	**Ние сме двама (трима, четирима).** ['niɛ smɛ 'dvama ('trima, ʧɛ'tirima)]

Smoking	**За пушачи** [za pu'ʃatʃi]
No smoking	**За непушачи** [za nɛpu'ʃatʃi]
Excuse me! (addressing a waiter)	**Ако обичате!** [akɔ ɔbitʃatɛ!]
menu	**меню** [mɛ'nju]
wine list	**Карта на виното** ['karta na 'vinɔtɔ]
The menu, please.	**Менюто, моля.** [mɛ'njutɔ, 'mɔʎa]

Are you ready to order?	**Готови ли сте да поръчате?** [gɔ'tɔvi li stɛ da pɔ'rəʧatɛ?]
What will you have?	**Какво ще поръчате?** [kak'vɔ ʃtɛ pɔ'rəʧatɛ?]
I'll have …	**Аз искам ….** [az 'iskam ….]

I'm a vegetarian.	**Аз съм вегетарианец /вегетарианка/.** [az səm vɛgɛtari'anɛc /vɛgɛtari'anka/]
meat	**месо** [mɛ'sɔ]
fish	**риба** ['riba]
vegetables	**зеленчуци** [zɛlen'ʧutsi]
Do you have vegetarian dishes?	**Имате ли вегетариански ястия?** ['imatɛ li vɛgɛtari'anski 'jastiʲa?]
I don't eat pork.	**Аз не ям свинско.** [az nɛ jam 'svinskɔ]
He /she/ doesn't eat meat.	**Той /тя/ не яде месо.** [tɔj /tʲa/ nɛ ja'dɛ mɛ'sɔ]
I am allergic to …	**Имам алергия към …** ['imam a'lergiʲa kəm …]

Would you please bring me ...

Донесете ми, моля ...
[dɔnɛ'sɛtɛ mi, 'mɔʎa ...]

salt | pepper | sugar

сол | пипер | захар
[sɔl | pi'pɛr | 'zahar]

coffee | tea | dessert

кафе | чай | десерт
[ka'fɛ | tʃaj | dɛ'sɛrt]

water | sparkling | plain

вода | газирана | негазирана
[vɔ'da | ga'zirana | nɛga'zirana]

a spoon | fork | knife

лъжица | вилица | нож
[lə'ʒica | 'vilica | nɔʒ]

a plate | napkin

чиния | салфетка
[tʃi'niʲa | sal'fɛtka]

Enjoy your meal!

Приятен апетит!
[pri'jatɛn apɛ'tit!]

One more, please.

Донесете още, моля.
[dɔnɛ'sɛtɛ 'ɔʃtɛ, 'mɔʎa]

It was very delicious.

Беше много вкусно.
['bɛʃɛ 'mnɔgɔ 'vkusnɔ]

check | change | tip

сметка | ресто | бакшиш
['smɛtka | 'rɛstɔ | bak'ʃiʃ]

Check, please.
(Could I have the check, please?)

Сметката, моля.
['smɛtkata, 'mɔʎa]

Can I pay by credit card?

Мога ли да платя с карта?
['mɔga li da pla'tʲa s 'karta?]

I'm sorry, there's a mistake here.

Извинявайте, тук има грешка.
[izvi'ɲavajtɛ, tuk 'ima 'grɛʃka]

Shopping

Can I help you?	**Мога ли да ви помогна?** ['mɔga li da vi pɔ'mɔgna?]
Do you have ...?	**Имате ли ...?** ['imatɛ li ...?]
I'm looking for ...	**Аз търся ...** [az 'tərsʲa ...]
I need ...	**Трябва ми ...** ['trʲabva mi ...]
I'm just looking.	**Само гледам.** ['samɔ 'gledam]
We're just looking.	**Ние само гледаме.** ['niɛ 'samɔ 'gledamɛ]
I'll come back later.	**Ще дойда по-късно.** [ʃtɛ 'dɔjda pɔ-'kəsnɔ]
We'll come back later.	**Ние ще дойдем по-късно.** ['niɛ ʃtɛ 'dɔjdɛm pɔ-'kəsnɔ]
discounts	sale	**намаления	разпродажба** [nama'leniʲa	razprɔ'daʒba]
Would you please show me ...	**Покажете ми, моля ...** [pɔka'ʒɛtɛ mi, 'mɔʎa ...]
Would you please give me ...	**Дайте ми, моля ...** ['dajtɛ mi, 'mɔʎa ...]
Can I try it on?	**Може ли да пробвам това?** ['mɔʒɛ li da 'prɔbvam tɔ'va?]
Excuse me, where's the fitting room?	**Извинявайте, къде може да пробвам това?** [izvi'ɲavajtɛ, kə'dɛ 'mɔʒɛ da 'prɔbvam tɔ'va?]
Which color would you like?	**Какъв цвят желаете?** [ka'kəv cvʲat ʒɛ'laɛtɛ?]
size	length	**размер	ръст** [raz'mɛr	rəst]
How does it fit?	**Стана ли ви?** ['stana li vi?]
How much is it?	**Колко струва това?** ['kɔlkɔ 'struva tɔ'va?]
That's too expensive.	**Това е много скъпо.** [tɔ'va ɛ 'mnɔgɔ 'skəpɔ]
I'll take it.	**Ще взема това.** [ʃtɛ 'vzɛma tɔ'va]

Excuse me, where do I pay?

Извинявайте, къде е касата?
[izvi'ɲavajtɛ, kə'dɛ ɛ 'kasata?]

Will you pay in cash or credit card?

Как ще плащате?
В брой или с карта?
[kak ʃtɛ 'plaʃtatɛ?
v brɔj 'ili s 'karta?]

In cash | with credit card

в брой | с карта
[v brɔj | s 'karta]

Do you want the receipt?

Трябва ли ви касов бон?
['trʲabva li vi 'kasɔv bɔn?]

Yes, please.

Да, бъдете така добър.
[da, bə'dɛtɛ ta'ka dɔ'bər]

No, it's OK.

Не, не трябва. Благодаря.
[nɛ, nɛ 'trʲabva. blagɔda'rʲa]

Thank you. Have a nice day!

Благодаря. Всичко хубаво!
[blagɔda'rʲa. 'vsitʃkɔ 'hubavɔ!]

In town

Excuse me, please.	**Извинете, моля ...** [izvi'nɛtɛ, 'mɔʎa ...]
I'm looking for ...	**Аз търся ...** [az 'tɤrsʲa ...]
the subway	**метрото** [mɛt'rɔtɔ]
my hotel	**хотела си** [hɔ'tɛla si]
the movie theater	**киното** ['kinɔtɔ]
a taxi stand	**стоянката на такси** [stɔ'jankata na 'taksi]
an ATM	**банкомат** [bankɔ'mat]
a foreign exchange office	**обмяна на валута** [ɔb'mʲana na va'luta]
an internet café	**интернет-кафе** [intɛr'nɛt-ka'fɛ]
... street	**улица ...** ['ulica ...]
this place	**ето това място** ['ɛtɔ tɔ'va 'mʲastɔ]
Do you know where ... is?	**Знаете ли, къде се намира ...?** ['znaɛtɛ li, kə'dɛ sɛ na'mira ...?]
Which street is this?	**Как се нарича тази улица?** [kak sɛ na'ritʃa 'tazi 'ulica?]
Show me where we are right now.	**Покажете, къде сме сега.** [pɔka'ʒɛtɛ, kə'dɛ smɛ sɛ'ga]
Can I get there on foot?	**Ще стигна ли дотам пеша?** [ʃtɛ 'stigna li dɔ'tam 'pɛʃa?]
Do you have a map of the city?	**Имате ли карта на града?** ['imatɛ li 'karta na gra'da?]
How much is a ticket to get in?	**Колко струва билет за вход?** ['kɔlkɔ 'struva bi'lɛt za vhɔd?]
Can I take pictures here?	**Тук може ли да се снима?** [tuk 'mɔʒɛ li da sɛ sni'ma?]
Are you open?	**Отворено ли е?** [ɔt'vɔrɛnɔ li ɛ?]

When do you open?

В колко отваряте?
[v 'kɔlkɔ ɔt'varʲatɛ?]

When do you close?

До колко часа работите?
[dɔ 'kɔlkɔ 'ʧasa 'rabɔtitɛ?]

Money

money	**пари** [pa'ri]
cash	**пари в брой** [pa'ri v brɔj]
paper money	**книжни пари** ['kniʒni pa'ri]
loose change	**дребни пари** [drɛbni pa'ri]
check | change | tip	**сметка | ресто | бакшиш** ['smɛtka | 'rɛstɔ | bak'ʃiʃ]
credit card	**кредитна карта** ['krɛditna 'karta]
wallet	**портмоне** [pɔrtmɔ'nɛ]
to buy	**да купя** [da 'kupʲa]
to pay	**да платя** [da pla'tʲa]
fine	**глоба** ['glɔba]
free	**безплатно** [bɛz'platnɔ]
Where can I buy …?	**Къде мога да купя …?** [kə'dɛ 'mɔga da 'kupʲa …?]
Is the bank open now?	**Отворена ли е банката сега ?** [ɔt'vɔrɛna li ɛ 'bankata sɛ'ga ?]
When does it open?	**В колко се отваря?** [v 'kɔlkɔ sɛ ɔt'varʲa?]
When does it close?	**До колко часа работи?** [dɔ 'kɔlkɔ 'tʃasa 'rabɔti?]
How much?	**Колко?** ['kɔlkɔ?]
How much is this?	**Колко струва?** ['kɔlkɔ 'struva?]
That's too expensive.	**Това е много скъпо.** [tɔ'va ɛ 'mnɔgɔ 'skəpɔ]
Excuse me, where do I pay?	**Извинявайте, къде е касата?** [izvi'ɲavajtɛ, kə'dɛ ɛ 'kasata?]
Check, please.	**Сметката, моля.** ['smɛtkata, 'mɔʎa]

Can I pay by credit card? | **Мога ли да платя с карта?**
['mɔga li da pla'tʲa s 'karta?]

Is there an ATM here? | **Тук има ли банкомат?**
[tuk 'ima li bankɔ'mat?]

I'm looking for an ATM. | **Трябва ми банкомат.**
['trʲabva mi bankɔ'mat]

I'm looking for a foreign exchange office. | **Аз търся обмяна на валута.**
[az 'tɤrsʲa ɔb'mʲana na va'luta]

I'd like to change … | **Бих искал да сменя …**
[bih 'iskal da smɛ'ɲa …]

What is the exchange rate? | **Какъв е курсът?**
[ka'kɤv ɛ 'kursɤt?]

Do you need my passport? | **Трябва ли ви паспортът ми?**
['trʲabva li vi pas'pɔrtɤt mi?]

Time

What time is it? | **Колко е часът?**
['kɔlkɔ ɛ ʧa'sət?]

When? | **Кога?**
[kɔ'ga?]

At what time? | **В колко?**
[v 'kɔlkɔ?]

now | later | after … | **сега | по-късно | след …**
[sɛ'ga | pɔ-'kəsnɔ | sled …]

---

one o'clock | **един часа**
[ɛ'din 'ʧasa]

one fifteen | **един часа и петнадесет минути**
[ɛ'din 'ʧasa i pɛt'nadɛsɛt mi'nuti]

one thirty | **един часа и тридесет минути**
[ɛ'din 'ʧasa i 'tridɛsɛt mi'nuti]

one forty-five | **два без петнадесет**
[dva bɛz pɛt'nadɛsɛt]

---

one | two | three | **един | два | три**
[ɛ'din | dva | tri]

four | five | six | **четири | пет | шест**
['ʧɛtiri | pɛt | ʃɛst]

seven | eight | nine | **седем | осем | девет**
['sɛdɛm | 'ɔsɛm | 'dɛvɛt]

ten | eleven | twelve | **десет | единадесет | дванадесет**
['dɛsɛt | ɛdi'nadɛsɛt | dva'nadɛsɛt]

---

in … | **след …**
[sled …]

five minutes | **пет минути**
[pɛt mi'nuti]

ten minutes | **десет минути**
['dɛsɛt mi'nuti]

fifteen minutes | **петнадесет минути**
[pɛt'nadɛsɛt mi'nuti]

twenty minutes | **двадесет минути**
['dvadɛsɛt mi'nuti]

---

half an hour | **половин час**
[pɔ'lɔvin ʧas]

an hour | **един час**
[ɛ'din ʧas]

in the morning

сутринта
[sut'rinta]

early in the morning

рано сутринта
['ranɔ sut'rinta]

this morning

днес сутринта
[dnɛs sut'rinta]

tomorrow morning

утре сутринта
['utrɛ sut'rinta]

at noon

на обяд
[na ɔb'jad]

in the afternoon

след обяд
[slɛd ɔ'bʲad]

in the evening

вечерта
[vɛtʃɛr'ta]

tonight

днес вечерта
[dnɛs vɛtʃɛr'ta]

at night

през нощта
[prɛz nɔ'ʃta]

yesterday

вчера
['vtʃɛra]

today

днес
[dnɛs]

tomorrow

утре
['utrɛ]

the day after tomorrow

вдругиден
['vdrugidɛn]

What day is it today?

Какъв ден е днес?
[ka'kəv dɛn ɛ dnɛs?]

It's ...

Днес е ...
[dnɛs ɛ ...]

Monday

понеделник
[pɔnɛ'dɛlnik]

Tuesday

вторник
['vtɔrnik]

Wednesday

сряда
['srʲada]

Thursday

четвъртък
[tʃɛt'vərtək]

Friday

петък
['pɛtək]

Saturday

събота
['səbɔta]

Sunday

неделя
[nɛ'dɛʎa]

Greetings. Introductions

Hello.
Здравейте.
[zdra'vɛjtɛ]

Pleased to meet you.
Радвам се, че се запознахме.
['radvam sɛ, tʃɛ sɛ zapɔz'nahmɛ]

Me too.
И аз.
[i az]

I'd like you to meet …
Запознайте се. Това е …
[zapɔ'znajtɛ sɛ. tɔ'va ɛ …]

Nice to meet you.
Много ми е приятно.
['mnɔgɔ mi ɛ pri'jatnɔ]

How are you?
Как сте?
[kak stɛ?]

My name is …
Казвам се …
['kazvam sɛ …]

His name is …
Той се казва …
[tɔj sɛ 'kazva …]

Her name is …
Тя се казва …
[tʲa sɛ 'kazva …]

What's your name?
Как се казвате?
[kak sɛ 'kazvatɛ?]

What's his name?
Как се казва той?
[kak sɛ 'kazva tɔj?]

What's her name?
Как се казва тя?
[kak sɛ 'kazva tʲa?]

What's your last name?
Как ви е фамилията?
[kak vi ɛ fa'miliʲata?]

You can call me …
Наричайте ме …
[na'ritʃajtɛ mɛ …]

Where are you from?
Откъде сте?
[ɔtkə'dɛ stɛ?]

I'm from …
Аз съм от …
[az səm ɔt …]

What do you do for a living?
Като какъв работите?
[ka'tɔ ka'kəv 'rabɔtitɛ?]

Who is this?
Кой сте?
[kɔj stɛ?]

Who is he?
Кой е той?
[kɔj ɛ tɔj?]

Who is she?
Коя е тя?
[kɔ'ja ɛ tʲa?]

Who are they?
Кои са те?
[kɔi sa tɛ?]

This is …

Това е …
[tɔ'va ɛ …]

my friend (masc.)

моят приятел
['mɔʲat pri'jatɛl]

my friend (fem.)

моята приятелка
['mɔʲata pri'jatɛlka]

my husband

моят мъж
['mɔʲat mɘʒ]

my wife

моята жена
['mɔʲata ʒɛ'na]

my father

моят баща
['mɔʲat ba'ʃta]

my mother

моята майка
['mɔʲata 'majka]

my brother

моят брат
['mɔʲat brat]

my sister

моята сестра
['mɔʲata sɛs'tra]

my son

моят син
['mɔʲat sin]

my daughter

моята дъщеря
['mɔʲata dɘʃtɛ'rʲa]

This is our son.

Това е нашият син.
[tɔ'va ɛ 'naʃiʲat sin]

This is our daughter.

Това е нашата дъщеря.
[tɔ'va ɛ 'naʃata dɘʃtɛ'rʲa]

These are my children.

Това са моите деца.
[tɔ'va sa 'mɔitɛ dɛ'tsa]

These are our children.

Това са нашите деца.
[tɔ'va sa 'naʃitɛ dɛ'tsa]

Farewells

Good bye!	**Довиждане!** [dɔ'viʒdanɛ!]
Bye! (inform.)	**Чао!** ['ʧaɔ!]
See you tomorrow.	**До утре!** [dɔ 'utrɛ!]
See you soon.	**До срещата!** [dɔ 'srɛʃtata!]
See you at seven.	**Ще се срещнем в седем.** [ʃtɛ sɛ 'srɛʃtnɛm v 'sɛdɛm]
Have fun!	**Забавлявайте се!** [zabav'ʎavajtɛ sɛ!]
Talk to you later.	**Ще поговорим по-късно.** [ʃtɛ pɔgɔ'vɔrim pɔ-'kəsnɔ]
Have a nice weekend.	**Успешен уикенд!** [us'pɛʃɛn u'ikɛnd!]
Good night.	**Лека нощ.** ['leka nɔʃt]
It's time for me to go.	**Сега трябва да тръгвам.** [sɛ'ga 'trʲabva da 'trəgvam]
I have to go.	**Трябва да тръгвам.** ['trʲabva da 'trəgvam]
I will be right back.	**Сега ще се върна.** [sɛ'ga ʃtɛ sɛ 'vərna]
It's late.	**Вече е късно.** ['vɛʧɛ ɛ 'kəsnɔ]
I have to get up early.	**Трябва рано да ставам.** ['trʲabva 'ranɔ da 'stavam]
I'm leaving tomorrow.	**Аз заминавам утре.** [az zami'navam 'utrɛ]
We're leaving tomorrow.	**Ние утре заминаваме.** ['niɛ 'utrɛ zami'navamɛ]
Have a nice trip!	**Щастливо пътуване!** [ʃtast'livɔ pə'tuvanɛ!]
It was nice meeting you.	**Беше ми приятно да се запознаем.** ['bɛʃɛ mi pri'jatnɔ da sɛ zapɔz'naɛm]
It was nice talking to you.	**Беше ми приятно да поговоря с вас.** ['bɛʃɛ mi pri'jatnɔ da pɔgɔ'vɔrʲa s vas]
Thanks for everything.	**Благодаря за всичко.** [blagɔda'rʲa za 'vsiʧkɔ]

I had a very good time.

Прекрасно прекарах времето.
[prɛk'rasnɔ prɛ'karah 'vrɛmɛtɔ]

We had a very good time.

Ние прекрасно прекарахме времето.
['niɛ prɛk'rasnɔ prɛ'karahmɛ 'vrɛmɛtɔ]

It was really great.

Всичкото беше страхотно.
[vsitʃkɔtɔ 'bɛʃɛ stra'hɔtnɔ]

I'm going to miss you.

Ще скучая.
[ʃtɛ sku'tʃaʲa]

We're going to miss you.

Ние ще скучаем.
['niɛ ʃtɛ sku'tʃaɛm]

Good luck!

Късмет! Успех!
[kəs'mɛt! us'pɛh!]

Say hi to …

Предайте поздрави на …
[prɛ'dajtɛ 'pɔzdravi na …]

Foreign language

I don't understand.	**Аз не разбирам.** [az nε raz'biram]
Write it down, please.	**Напишете това, моля.** [napi'ʃεtε tɔ'va, 'mɔʎa]
Do you speak …?	**Знаете ли …?** ['znaεtε li …?]
I speak a little bit of …	**Малко знам …** ['malkɔ znam …]
English	**английски** [ang'lijski]
Turkish	**турски** ['turski]
Arabic	**арабски** [a'rabski]
French	**френски** ['frεnski]
German	**немски** ['nεmski]
Italian	**италиански** [itali'anski]
Spanish	**испански** [is'panski]
Portuguese	**португалски** [pɔrtu'galski]
Chinese	**китайски** [ki'tajski]
Japanese	**японски** [ja'pɔnski]
Can you repeat that, please.	**Повторете, моля.** [pɔvtɔ'rεtε, 'mɔʎa]
I understand.	**Аз разбирам.** [az raz'biram]
I don't understand.	**Аз не разбирам.** [az nε raz'biram]
Please speak more slowly.	**Говорете по-бавно, моля.** [gɔ'vɔrεtε pɔ-'bavnɔ, 'mɔʎa]
Is that correct? (Am I saying it right?)	**Това правилно ли е?** [tɔ'va 'pravilnɔ li ε?]
What is this? (What does this mean?)	**Какво е това?** [kak'vɔ ε tɔ'va?]

Apologies

Excuse me, please.

Извинете, моля.
[izvi'nɛtɛ, 'mɔʎa]

I'm sorry.

Съжалявам.
[səʒa'ʎavam]

I'm really sorry.

Много съжалявам.
['mnɔgɔ səʒa'ʎavam]

Sorry, it's my fault.

Виновен съм, вината е моя.
[vi'nɔvɛn səm, vi'nata ɛ mɔ'a]

My mistake.

Грешката е моя.
['grɛʃkata ɛ 'mɔ'a]

May I ...?

Мога ли ...?
['mɔga li ...?]

Do you mind if I ...?

Имате ли нещо против, ако аз ...?
['imatɛ li 'nɛʃtɔ prɔ'tiv, a'kɔ az ...?]

It's OK.

Няма нищо.
['ɲama 'niʃtɔ]

It's all right.

Всичко е наред.
[vsitʃkɔ ɛ na'rɛd]

Don't worry about it.

Не се безпокойте.
[nɛ sɛ bɛzpɔ'kojtɛ]

Agreement

Yes.	**Да.**
	[da]
Yes, sure.	**Да, разбира се.**
	[da, raz'bira sɛ]
OK (Good!)	**Добре!**
	[dɔb'rɛ!]
Very well.	**Много добре!**
	['mnɔgɔ dɔb'rɛ!]
Certainly!	**Разбира се!**
	[raz'bira sɛ!]
I agree.	**Съгласен /съгласна/ съм.**
	[səg'lasɛn /səg'lasna/ səm]

That's correct.	**Вярно.**
	['vʲarnɔ]
That's right.	**Правилно.**
	['pravilnɔ]
You're right.	**Прав /права/ сте.**
	[prav /'prava/ stɛ]
I don't mind.	**Не възразявам.**
	[nɛ vəzra'zʲavam]
Absolutely right.	**Абсолютно вярно.**
	[absɔ'ljutnɔ 'vʲarnɔ]

It's possible.	**Това е възможно.**
	[tɔ'va ɛ vəz'mɔʒnɔ]
That's a good idea.	**Това е добра идея.**
	[tɔ'va ɛ dɔ'bra i'dɛʲa]
I can't say no.	**Не мога да откажа.**
	[nɛ 'mɔga da ɔt'kaʒa]
I'd be happy to.	**Ще се радвам.**
	[ʃtɛ sɛ 'radvam]
With pleasure.	**С удоволствие.**
	[s udɔ'vɔlstviɛ]

Refusal. Expressing doubt

No.	**Не.** [nɛ]
Certainly not.	**Не, разбира се.** [nɛ, raz'bira sɛ]
I don't agree.	**Аз не съм съгласен /съгласна/.** [az nɛ səm səg'lasɛn /səg'lasna/]
I don't think so.	**Аз не мисля така.** [az nɛ 'misʎa ta'ka]
It's not true.	**Това не е вярно.** [to'va nɛ ɛ 'vʲarnɔ]
You are wrong.	**Грешите.** [grɛ'ʃitɛ]
I think you are wrong.	**Мисля, че грешите.** ['misʎa, ʧɛ grɛ'ʃitɛ]
I'm not sure.	**Не съм сигурен /сигурна/.** [nɛ səm 'sigurɛn /'sigurna/]
It's impossible.	**Това не е възможно.** [to'va nɛ ɛ vəz'mɔʒnɔ]
Nothing of the kind (sort)!	**Нищо подобно!** ['niʃtɔ pɔ'dɔbnɔ!]
The exact opposite.	**Напротив!** [na'prɔtiv!]
I'm against it.	**Аз съм против.** [az səm prɔ'tiv]
I don't care.	**На мен ми е все едно.** [na mɛn mi ɛ vsɛ ɛd'nɔ]
I have no idea.	**Нямам представа.** ['ɲamam prɛd'stava]
I doubt that.	**Съмнявам се, че е така.** [səm'ɲavam sɛ, ʧɛ ɛ ta'ka]
Sorry, I can't.	**Извинете ме, аз не мога.** [izvi'nɛtɛ mɛ, az nɛ 'mɔga]
Sorry, I don't want to.	**Извинете ме, аз не искам.** [izvi'nɛtɛ mɛ, az nɛ 'iskam]
Thank you, but I don't need this.	**Благодаря, това не ми трябва.** [blagɔda'rʲa, tɔ'va nɛ mi 'trʲabva]
It's late.	**Вече е късно.** ['vɛʧɛ ɛ 'kəsnɔ]

I have to get up early.

Трябва рано да ставам.
['trʲabva 'ranɔ da 'stavam]

I don't feel well.

Чувствам се зле.
[ʧuvstvam sɛ zle]

Expressing gratitude

Thank you.	**Благодаря.** [blagɔda'rʲa]
Thank you very much.	**Много благодаря.** [mnɔgɔ blagɔda'rʲa]
I really appreciate it.	**Много съм признателен /признателна/.** ['mnɔgɔ səm priz'natɛlɛn /priz'natɛlna/]
I'm really grateful to you.	**Много съм ви благодарен /благодарна/.** ['mnɔgɔ səm vi blagɔ'darɛn /blagɔ'darna/]
We are really grateful to you.	**Ние сме ви благодарни.** ['niɛ smɛ vi blagɔ'darni]
Thank you for your time.	**Благодаря ви, че отделихте време.** [blagɔda'rʲa vi, ʧɛ ɔtdɛ'lihtɛ 'vrɛmɛ]
Thanks for everything.	**Благодаря за всичко.** [blagɔda'rʲa za 'vsiʧkɔ]
Thank you for ...	**Благодаря за ...** [blagɔda'rʲa za ...]
your help	**вашата помощ** ['vaʃata 'pɔmɔʃt]
a nice time	**хубавото време** ['hubavɔtɔ 'vrɛmɛ]
a wonderful meal	**чудната храна** ['ʧudnata hra'na]
a pleasant evening	**приятната вечер** [pri'jatnata 'vɛʧɛr]
a wonderful day	**прекрасния ден** [prɛk'rasnʲa dɛn]
an amazing journey	**интересната екскурзия** [intɛ'rɛsnata ɛks'kurziʲa]
Don't mention it.	**Няма за що.** ['ɲama za ʃtɔ]
You are welcome.	**Моля.** ['mɔʎa]
Any time.	**Винаги моля.** ['vinagi 'mɔʎa]
My pleasure.	**Радвам се, че помогнах.** ['radvam sɛ, ʧɛ pɔ'mɔgnah]

Forget it. It's alright.

Забравете.
[zabra'vɛtɛ]

Don't worry about it.

Не се безпокойте.
[nɛ sɛ bɛzpɔ'kɔjtɛ]

Congratulations. Best wishes

Congratulations!
Поздравявам!
[pɔzdra'vʲavam!]

Happy birthday!
Честит рожден ден!
[ʧɛs'tit rɔʒ'dɛn dɛn!]

Merry Christmas!
Весела Коледа!
['vɛsɛla 'kɔleda!]

Happy New Year!
Честита Нова година!
[ʧɛs'tita 'nɔva gɔ'dina!]

Happy Easter!
Честит Великден!
[ʧɛs'tit vɛ'likdɛn!]

Happy Hanukkah!
Честита Ханука!
[ʧɛs'tita 'hanuka!]

I'd like to propose a toast.
Имам тост.
['imam tɔst]

Cheers!
За вашето здраве!
[za 'vaʃɛtɔ 'zdravɛ!]

Let's drink to ...!
Да пием за ...!
[da pi'ɛm za ...!]

To our success!
За нашия успех!
[za 'naʃʲʲa us'pɛh!]

To your success!
За вашия успех!
[za 'vaʃʲʲa us'pɛh!]

Good luck!
Късмет!
[kəs'mɛt!]

Have a nice day!
Приятен ден!
[pri'jatɛn dɛn!]

Have a good holiday!
Хубава почивка!
['hubava pɔ'ʧivka!]

Have a safe journey!
Успешно пътуване!
[us'pɛʃnɔ pə'tuvanɛ!]

I hope you get better soon!
Желая ви скорошно оздравяване!
[ʒɛ'laʲa vi 'skɔrɔʃnɔ ɔzdra'vʲavanɛ!]

Socializing

Why are you sad?	**Защо сте разстроени?** [za'ʃtɔ stɛ raz'strɔɛni?]
Smile! Cheer up!	**Усмихнете се!** [usmih'nɛtɛ sɛ!]
Are you free tonight?	**Заети ли сте днес вечерта?** [za'ɛti li stɛ dnɛs vɛtʃɛr'ta?]
May I offer you a drink?	**Мога ли да ви предложа едно питие?** ['mɔga li da vi prɛd'lɔʒa ɛd'nɔ piti'ɛ?]
Would you like to dance?	**Искате ли да танцувате?** ['iskatɛ li da tan'tsuvatɛ?]
Let's go to the movies.	**Да отидем ли на кино?** [da ɔ'tidɛm li na 'kinɔ?]
May I invite you to ...?	**Мога ли да ви поканя на ...?** ['mɔga li da vi pɔ'kaɲa na ...?]
a restaurant	**ресторант** [rɛstɔ'rant]
the movies	**кино** ['kinɔ]
the theater	**театър** [tɛ'atər]
go for a walk	**на разходка** [na raz'hɔdka]
At what time?	**В колко?** [v 'kɔlkɔ?]
tonight	**днес вечерта** [dnɛs vɛtʃɛr'ta]
at six	**в 6 часа** [v ʃɛst tʃasa]
at seven	**в 7 часа** [v 'sɛdɛm tʃasa]
at eight	**в 8 часа** [v 'ɔsɛm tʃasa]
at nine	**в 9 часа** [v 'dɛvɛt tʃasa]
Do you like it here?	**Харесва ли ви тук?** [ha'rɛsva li vi tuk?]
Are you here with someone?	**С някой ли сте тук?** [s 'ɲakɔj li stɛ tuk?]

I'm with my friend. | **Аз съм с приятел /приятелка/.**
[az səm s pri'jatɛl /pri'jatɛlka/]

I'm with my friends. | **Аз съм с приятели.**
[az səm s pri'jatɛli]

No, I'm alone. | **Аз съм сам /сама/.**
[az səm sam /sa'ma/]

Do you have a boyfriend? | **Имаш ли приятел?**
['imaʃ li pri'jatɛl?]

I have a boyfriend. | **Аз имам приятел.**
[az 'imam pri'jatɛl]

Do you have a girlfriend? | **Имаш ли приятелка?**
['imaʃ li pri'jatɛlka?]

I have a girlfriend. | **Аз имам гадже.**
[az 'imam 'gadʒɛ]

Can I see you again? | **Ще се видим ли още?**
[ʃtɛ sɛ 'vidim li ɔ'ʃtɛ?]

Can I call you? | **Мога ли да ти се обадя?**
['mɔga li da ti sɛ ɔ'badia?]

Call me. (Give me a call.) | **Обади ми се.**
[ɔ'badi mi sɛ]

What's your number? | **Какъв ти е номерът?**
[ka'kəv ti ɛ 'nɔmɛrət?]

I miss you. | **Липсваш ми.**
['lipsvaʃ mi]

You have a beautiful name. | **Имате много красиво име.**
['imatɛ 'mnɔgɔ kra'sivɔ imɛ]

I love you. | **Аз те обичам.**
[az tɛ ɔ'bitʃam]

Will you marry me? | **Омъжи се за мен.**
[ɔ'məʒi sɛ za mɛn]

You're kidding! | **Шегувате се!**
[ʃɛ'guvatɛ sɛ!]

I'm just kidding. | **Аз само се шегувам.**
[az 'samɔ sɛ ʃɛ'guvam]

Are you serious? | **Сериозно ли говорите?**
[sɛri'ɔznɔ li gɔ'vɔritɛ?]

I'm serious. | **Сериозен /сериозна/ съм.**
[sɛri'ɔzɛn /sɛri'ɔzna/ səm]

Really?! | **Наистина ли?!**
[na'istina li?!]

It's unbelievable! | **Това е невероятно!**
[tɔ'va ɛ nɛvɛrɔ'jatnɔ!]

I don't believe you. | **Не ви вярвам.**
[nɛ vi 'viarvam]

I can't. | **Аз не мога.**
[az nɛ 'mɔga]

I don't know. | **Аз не знам.**
[az nɛ znam]

I don't understand you.

Аз не ви разбирам.
[az nɛ vi raz'biram]

Please go away.

Вървете си, моля.
[vər'vɛtɛ si, 'mɔʎa]

Leave me alone!

Оставете ме на мира!
[ɔs'tavɛtɛ mɛ na mi'ra!]

I can't stand him.

Не го понасям.
[nɛ gɔ pɔ'nasʲam]

You are disgusting!

Отвратителен сте!
[ɔtvra'titɛlen stɛ!]

I'll call the police!

Ще повикам полиция!
[ʃtɛ 'pɔvikam pɔ'litsiʲa!]

Sharing impressions. Emotions

I like it.	**Това ми харесва.** [to'va mi ha'rɛsva]
Very nice.	**Много мило.** ['mnɔgɔ 'milɔ]
That's great!	**Това е страхотно!** [to'va ɛ stra'hotnɔ!]
It's not bad.	**Не е лошо.** [nɛ ɛ 'lɔʃɔ]
I don't like it.	**Това не ми харесва.** [to'va nɛ mi ha'rɛsva]
It's not good.	**Това не е добре.** [to'va nɛ ɛ do'brɛ]
It's bad.	**Това е лошо.** [to'va ɛ 'lɔʃɔ]
It's very bad.	**Това е много лошо.** [to'va ɛ 'mnɔgɔ 'lɔʃɔ]
It's disgusting.	**Това е отвратително.** [to'va ɛ ɔtvra'titɛlnɔ]
I'm happy.	**Щастлив /щастлива/ съм.** [ʃtast'liv /ʃtast'liva/ səm]
I'm content.	**Доволен /доволна/ съм.** [do'vɔlen /dɔ'vɔlna/ səm]
I'm in love.	**Влюбен /влюбена/ съм.** [vljubɛn /'vljubɛna/ səm]
I'm calm.	**Спокоен /спокойна/ съм.** [spɔ'kɔɛn /spɔ'kɔjna/ səm]
I'm bored.	**Скучно ми е.** ['skutʃnɔ mi ɛ]
I'm tired.	**Аз се измории.** [az sɛ izmɔ'rih]
I'm sad.	**Тъжно ми е.** ['təʒnɔ mi ɛ]
I'm frightened.	**Уплашен /уплашена/ съм.** [up'laʃɛn /up'laʃɛna/ səm]
I'm angry.	**Ядосвам се.** [ja'dɔsvam sɛ]
I'm worried.	**Вълнувам се.** [vəl'nuvam sɛ]
I'm nervous.	**Аз нервнича.** [az 'nɛrvnitʃa]

I'm jealous. (envious)

Аз завиждам.
[az za'viʒdam]

I'm surprised.

Учуден /учудена/ съм.
[u'tʃudɛn /u'tʃudɛna/ səm]

I'm perplexed.

Аз съм объркан /объркана/.
[az səm ɔ'bərkan /ɔ'bərkana/]

Problems. Accidents

I've got a problem.
Аз имам проблем.
[az 'imam prɔb'lem]

We've got a problem.
Ние имаме проблем.
['niɛ 'imamɛ prɔb'lem]

I'm lost.
Аз се заблудих.
[az sɛ zab'ludih]

I missed the last bus (train).
Аз закъснях за последния автобус (влак).
[az zakəs'ɲah za pɔs'lednɪʲa avtɔ'bus (vlak)]

I don't have any money left.
Не ми останаха никакви пари.
[nɛ mi ɔs'tanaha 'nikakvi pa'ri]

I've lost my ...
Аз загубих ...
[az za'gubih ...]

Someone stole my ...
Откраднаха ми ...
[ɔtk'radnaha mi ...]

passport
паспорта
[pas'pɔrta]

wallet
портмонето
[pɔrtmɔ'nɛtɔ]

papers
документите
[dɔku'mɛntitɛ]

ticket
билета
[bi'leta]

money
парите
[pa'ritɛ]

handbag
чантата
['tʃantata]

camera
фотоапарата
[fɔtɔapa'rata]

laptop
лаптопа
[lap'tɔpa]

tablet computer
таблета
[tab'leta]

mobile phone
телефона
[tɛle'fɔna]

Help me!
Помогнете!
[pɔmɔg'nɛtɛ!]

What's happened?
Какво се случи?
[kak'vɔ sɛ slu'tʃi?]

fire	**пожар** [pɔˈʒar]
shooting	**стрелба** [strɛlˈba]
murder	**убийство** [uˈbijstvɔ]
explosion	**взрив** [vzriv]
fight	**бой** [bɔj]

Call the police!	**Извикайте полиция!** [izviˈkajtɛ pɔˈlitsiʲa!]
Please hurry up!	**Моля, по-бързо!** [ˈmɔʎa, pɔ-ˈbərzɔ!]
I'm looking for the police station.	**Аз търся полицейски участък.** [az ˈtərsʲa pɔliˈtsɛjski uˈtʃastək]
I need to make a call.	**Трябва да се обадя.** [ˈtrʲabva da sɛ ɔˈbadʲa]
May I use your phone?	**Мога ли да се обадя?** [ˈmɔga li da sɛ ɔˈbadʲa?]

I've been …	**Мен ме …** [mɛn mɛ …]
mugged	**ограбиха** [ɔgˈrabiha]
robbed	**обраха** [ɔbˈraha]
raped	**изнасилиха** [iznaˈsiliha]
attacked (beaten up)	**пребиха** [prɛˈbiha]

Are you all right?	**Всичко ли е наред?** [ˈvsitʃkɔ li ɛ naˈrɛd?]
Did you see who it was?	**Видяхте ли, кой беше?** [viˈdʲahtɛ li, kɔj ˈbɛʃɛ?]
Would you be able to recognize the person?	**Ще можете ли да го познаете?** [ʃtɛ ˈmɔʒɛtɛ li da gɔ pɔzˈnaɛtɛ?]
Are you sure?	**Сигурен /сигурна/ ли сте?** [ˈsigurɛn /ˈsigurna/ li stɛ?]

Please calm down.	**Моля, да се успокоите.** [ˈmɔʎa, da sɛ uspɔˈkɔitɛ]
Take it easy!	**По-спокойно!** [pɔ-spɔˈkɔjnɔ!]
Don't worry!	**Не се безпокойте.** [nɛ sɛ bɛzpɔˈkɔjtɛ]
Everything will be fine.	**Всичко ще се оправи.** [ˈvsitʃkɔ ʃtɛ sɛ ɔpˈravi]
Everything's all right.	**Всичко е наред.** [ˈvsitʃkɔ ɛ naˈrɛd]

Come here, please.

Елате, моля.
[ɛ'latɛ, 'mɔʎa]

I have some questions for you.

Имам няколко въпроса към Вас.
['imam ɲa'kɔlkɔ vəp'rɔsa kəm vas]

Wait a moment, please.

Изчакайте, моля.
[iz'tʃakajtɛ, 'mɔʎa]

Do you have any I.D.?

Имате ли документи?
['imatɛ li dɔku'mɛnti?]

Thanks. You can leave now.

Благодаря. Свободни сте.
[blagɔda'rʲa. svɔ'bɔdni stɛ]

Hands behind your head!

Ръцете зад тила!
[rə'tsɛtɛ zad 'tila!]

You're under arrest!

Арестуван /арестувана/ сте!
[arɛs'tuvan /arɛs'tuvana/ stɛ!]

Health problems

Please help me.
Помогнете, моля.
[pɔmɔg'nɛtɛ, 'mɔʎa]

I don't feel well.
Лошо ми е.
['lɔʃɔ mi ɛ]

My husband doesn't feel well.
На мъжа ми му е лошо.
[na mə'ʒa mi mu ɛ 'lɔʃɔ]

My son ...
На сина ми ...
[na si'na mi ...]

My father ...
На баща ми ...
[na ba'ʃta mi ...]

My wife doesn't feel well.
На жена ми и е лошо.
[na ʒɛ'na mi i ɛ 'lɔʃɔ]

My daughter ...
На дъщеря ми ...
[na dəʃtɛr'ja mi ...]

My mother ...
На майка ми ...
[na 'majka mi ...]

I've got a ...
Боли ме ...
[bɔ'li mɛ ...]

headache
главата
[gla'vata]

sore throat
гърлото
['gərlɔtɔ]

stomach ache
корема
[kɔ'rɛma]

toothache
зъба
['zəba]

I feel dizzy.
Ви е ми се свят.
[vi ɛ mi sɛ sv'at]

He has a fever.
Той има температура.
[tɔj 'ima tɛmpɛra'tura]

She has a fever.
Тя има температура.
[t'a 'ima tɛmpɛra'tura]

I can't breathe.
Аз не мога да дишам.
[az nɛ 'mɔga da 'diʃam]

I'm short of breath.
Аз се задъхвам.
[az sɛ za'dəhvam]

I am asthmatic.
Аз съм астматик.
[az səm astma'tik]

I am diabetic.
Аз съм диабетик.
[az səm diabɛ'tik]

I can't sleep.

Имам безсъние.
['imam bɛz'səniɛ]

food poisoning

хранително отравяне
[hra'nitɛlnɔ ɔt'ravʲanɛ]

It hurts here.

Тук ме боли.
[tuk mɛ bɔ'li]

Help me!

Помогнете!
[pɔmɔg'nɛtɛ!]

I am here!

Аз съм тук!
[az səm tuk!]

We are here!

Ние сме тук!
['niɛ smɛ tuk!]

Get me out of here!

Извадете ме!
[izva'dɛtɛ mɛ!]

I need a doctor.

Трябва ми лекар.
['trʲabva mi 'lekar]

I can't move.

Не мога да мърдам.
[nɛ 'mɔga da 'mərdam]

I can't move my legs.

Не си чувствам краката.
[nɛ si 'tʃuvstvam kra'kata]

I have a wound.

Аз съм ранен /ранена/.
[az səm 'ranɛn /'ranɛna/]

Is it serious?

Сериозно ли е?
[sɛri'ɔznɔ li ɛ?]

My documents are in my pocket.

Документите ми са в джоба.
[dɔku'mɛntitɛ mi sa v 'dʒɔba]

Calm down!

Успокойте се!
[uspɔ'kɔjtɛ sɛ!]

May I use your phone?

Мога ли да се обадя?
['mɔga li da sɛ ɔ'badʲa?]

Call an ambulance!

Повикайте бърза помощ!
[pɔvi'kajtɛ 'bərza 'pɔmɔʃt!]

It's urgent!

Това е спешно!
[tɔ'va ɛ 'spɛʃnɔ!]

It's an emergency!

Това е много спешно!
[tɔ'va ɛ 'mnɔgɔ 'spɛʃnɔ!]

Please hurry up!

Моля, по-бързо!
['mɔʎa, pɔ-'bərzɔ!]

Would you please call a doctor?

Повикайте лекар, моля.
[pɔvi'kajtɛ 'lekar, 'mɔʎa]

Where is the hospital?

Кажете, моля, къде е болницата?
[ka'ʒɛtɛ, 'mɔʎa, kə'dɛ ɛ 'bɔlnitsata?]

How are you feeling?

Как се чувствате?
[kak sɛ 'tʃuvstvatɛ?]

Are you all right?

Всичко ли е наред?
['vsitʃkɔ li ɛ na'rɛd?]

What's happened?

Какво се случи?
[kak'vɔ sɛ slu'tʃi?]

I feel better now.

Вече ми е по-добре.
['vɛʧɛ mi ɛ pɔ-dɔbrɛ]

It's OK.

Всичко е наред.
[vsiʧkɔ ɛ naˈrɛd]

It's all right.

Всичко е наред.
[vsiʧkɔ ɛ naˈrɛd]

At the pharmacy

pharmacy (drugstore)	**аптека** [ap'tɛka]
24-hour pharmacy	**денонощна аптека** [dɛnɔ'nɔʃtna ap'tɛka]
Where is the closest pharmacy?	**Къде е най-близката аптека?** [kə'dɛ ɛ naj-'blizkata ap'tɛka?]
Is it open now?	**Сега отворена ли е?** [sɛ'ga ɔt'vɔrɛna li ɛ?]
At what time does it open?	**В колко се отваря?** [v 'kɔlkɔ sɛ ɔt'variʲa?]
At what time does it close?	**До колко работи?** [dɔ 'kɔlkɔ 'rabɔti?]
Is it far?	**Далече ли е?** [da'lɛtʃɛ li ɛ?]
Can I get there on foot?	**Ще стигна ли дотам пеша?** [ʃtɛ 'stigna li dɔ'tam 'pɛʃa?]
Can you show me on the map?	**Покажете ми на картата, моля.** [pɔka'ʒɛtɛ mi na 'kartata, 'mɔʎa]
Please give me something for ...	**Дайте ми нещо за ...** ['dajtɛ mi 'nɛʃtɔ za ...]
a headache	**главоболие** [glavɔ'bɔliɛ]
a cough	**кашлица** ['kaʃlitsa]
a cold	**настинка** [nas'tinka]
the flu	**грип** [grip]
a fever	**температура** [tɛmpɛra'tura]
a stomach ache	**болки в стомаха** ['bɔlki v stɔ'maha]
nausea	**повръщане** [pɔv'rəʃtanɛ]
diarrhea	**диария** [di'ariʲa]
constipation	**запек** ['zapɛk]
pain in the back	**болки в гърба** ['bɔlki v 'gərba]

chest pain	**болки в гърдите** ['bɔlki v gər'ditɛ]
side stitch	**болки отстрани** ['bɔlki ɔtstra'ni]
abdominal pain	**болки в корема** ['bɔlki v kɔ'rɛma]

pill	**таблетка** [tab'letka]
ointment, cream	**маз, мехлем, крем** [maz, mɛh'lem, krɛm]
syrup	**сироп** [si'rɔp]
spray	**спрей** [sprɛj]
drops	**капки** ['kapki]

You need to go to the hospital.	**Трябва да отидете в болница.** ['trʲabva da ɔti'dɛtɛ v 'bɔlnitsa]
health insurance	**застраховка** [zastra'hɔvka]
prescription	**рецепта** [rɛ'tsɛpta]
insect repellant	**препарат от насекоми** [prɛpa'rat ɔt nasɛ'kɔmi]
Band Aid	**лейкопласт** [lejkɔ'plast]

The bare minimum

Excuse me, ...	**Извинете, ...** [izvi'nɛtɛ, ...]
Hello.	**Здравейте.** [zdra'vɛjtɛ]
Thank you.	**Благодаря.** [blagɔda'rʲa]
Good bye.	**Довиждане.** [dɔ'viʒdanɛ]
Yes.	**Да.** [da]
No.	**Не.** [nɛ]
I don't know.	**Аз не знам.** [az nɛ znam]
Where?	Where to?	When?	**Къде?	Накъде?	Кога?** [kə'dɛ?	nakə'dɛ?	kɔ'ga?]
I need ...	**Трябва ми ...** ['trʲabva mi ...]
I want ...	**Аз искам ...** [az 'iskam ...]
Do you have ...?	**Имате ли ...?** ['imatɛ li ...?]
Is there a ... here?	**Тук има ли ...?** [tuk 'ima li ...?]
May I ...?	**Мога ли ...?** ['mɔga li ...?]
..., please (polite request)	**Моля.** ['mɔʎa]
I'm looking for ...	**Аз търся ...** [az 'tərsʲa ...]
restroom	**тоалетна** [tɔa'lɛtna]
ATM	**банкомат** [bankɔ'mat]
pharmacy (drugstore)	**аптека** [ap'tɛka]
hospital	**болница** ['bɔlnitsa]
police station	**полицейски участък** [pɔli'tsɛjski u'ʧastək]
subway	**метро** [mɛt'rɔ]

taxi	**такси**
	['taksi]
train station	**гара**
	['gara]

My name is …	**Казвам се …**
	['kazvam sɛ …]
What's your name?	**Как се казвате?**
	[kak sɛ 'kazvatɛ?]
Could you please help me?	**Помогнете ми, моля.**
	[pɔmɔg'nɛtɛ mi, 'mɔʎa]
I've got a problem.	**Аз имам проблем.**
	[az 'imam prɔb'lem]
I don't feel well.	**Лошо ми е.**
	['lɔʃɔ mi ɛ]
Call an ambulance!	**Повикайте бърза помощ!**
	[pɔvi'kajtɛ 'bərza 'pɔmɔʃt!]
May I make a call?	**Може ли да се обадя?**
	['mɔʒɛ li da sɛ ɔ'badʲa?]

I'm sorry.	**Извинявам се.**
	[izvi'ɲavam sɛ]
You're welcome.	**Моля.**
	['mɔʎa]

I, me	**аз**
	[az]
you (inform.)	**ти**
	[ti]
he	**той**
	[tɔj]
she	**тя**
	[tʲa]
they (masc.)	**те**
	[tɛ]
they (fem.)	**те**
	[tɛ]
we	**ние**
	['niɛ]
you (pl)	**вие**
	['viɛ]
you (sg, form.)	**Вие**
	['viɛ]

ENTRANCE	**ВХОД**
	[vhɔd]
EXIT	**ИЗХОД**
	['izhɔd]
OUT OF ORDER	**НЕ РАБОТИ**
	[nɛ 'rabɔti]
CLOSED	**ЗАТВОРЕНО**
	[zat'vɔrɛnɔ]

OPEN **ОТВОРЕНО**
[ɔt'vɔrɛnɔ]

FOR WOMEN **ЗА ЖЕНИ**
[za ʒɛ'ni]

FOR MEN **ЗА МЪЖЕ**
[za mə'ʒɛ]

BOOKS

T&P

CONCISE
DICTIONARY

This section contains more
than 1,500 useful words
arranged alphabetically.
The dictionary includes a lot
of gastronomic terms and
will be helpful when ordering
food at a restaurant or buying
groceries

T&P Books Publishing

DICTIONARY CONTENTS

T&P Books Publishing

T&P Books Publishing

time	**време** (с)	[v'rɛmɛ]
hour	**час** (м)	[tʃas]
half an hour	**половин час** (м)	[pɔlɔ'vin tʃas]
minute	**минута** (ж)	[mi'nuta]
second	**секунда** (ж)	[sɛ'kunda]
today (adv)	**днес**	[dnɛs]
tomorrow (adv)	**утре**	['utrɛ]
yesterday (adv)	**вчера**	[v'tʃəra]
Monday	**понеделник** (м)	[pɔnɛ'dɛlnik]
Tuesday	**вторник** (м)	[f'tɔrnik]
Wednesday	**сряда** (ж)	[s'rʲada]
Thursday	**четвъртък** (м)	[tʃɛt'vɪrtɪk]
Friday	**петък** (м)	['pɛtɪk]
Saturday	**събота** (ж)	['sɪbɔta]
Sunday	**неделя** (ж)	[nɛ'dɛʎa]
day	**ден** (м)	[dɛn]
working day	**работен ден** (м)	[ra'bɔtɛn dɛn]
public holiday	**празничен ден** (м)	[p'raznitʃən dɛn]
weekend	**почивни дни** (м мн)	[pɔ'tʃivni dni]
week	**седмица** (ж)	['sɛdmitsa]
last week (adv)	**през миналата седмица**	[prɛs 'minalata 'sɛdmitsa]
next week (adv)	**през следващата седмица**	[prɛs s'lɛdvaʃtata 'sɛdmitsa]
sunrise	**изгрев слънце** (с)	['izgrɛv s'lɪntsə]
sunset	**залез** (м)	['zalɛz]
in the morning	**сутринта**	[sutrin'ta]
in the afternoon	**следобед**	[slɛ'dɔbɛd]
in the evening	**вечер**	['vɛtʃər]
tonight (this evening)	**довечера**	[dɔ'vɛtʃəra]
at night	**нощем**	['nɔʃtɛm]
midnight	**полунощ** (ж)	[pɔlu'nɔʃt]
January	**януари** (м)	[jɑnu'ari]
February	**февруари** (м)	[fɛvru'ari]
March	**март** (м)	[mart]
April	**април** (м)	[ap'ril]
May	**май** (м)	[maj]

June	юни (м)	['juni]
July	юли (м)	['juli]
August	август (м)	['avgust]
September	септември (м)	[sɛp'tɛmvri]
October	октомври (м)	[ɔk'tɔmvri]
November	ноември (м)	[nɔ'ɛmvri]
December	декември (м)	[dɛ'kɛmvri]

in spring	през пролетта	[prɛz prɔlɛt'ta]
in summer	през лятото	[prɛz 'ʎatoto]
in fall	през есента	[prɛz ɛsɛn'ta]
in winter	през зимата	[prɛz 'zimata]

month	месец (м)	['mɛsɛʦ]
season (summer, etc.)	сезон (м)	[sɛ'zɔn]
year	година (ж)	[gɔ'dina]
century	век (м)	[vɛk]

2. Numbers. Numerals

digit, figure	цифра (ж)	['ʦifra]
number	число (с)	[ʧis'lɔ]
minus sign	минус (м)	['minus]
plus sign	плюс (м)	[plys]
sum, total	сума (ж)	['suma]

first (adj)	първи	['pɪrvi]
second (adj)	втори	[f'tɔri]
third (adj)	трети	[t'rɛti]

0 zero	нула (ж)	['nula]
1 one	едно	[ɛd'nɔ]
2 two	две	[dvɛ]
3 three	три	[tri]
4 four	четири	['ʧətiri]

5 five	пет	[pɛt]
6 six	шест	[ʃɛst]
7 seven	седем	['sɛdɛm]
8 eight	осем	['ɔsɛm]
9 nine	девет	['dɛvɛt]
10 ten	десет	['dɛsɛt]

11 eleven	единадесет	[ɛdi'nadɛsɛt]
12 twelve	дванадесет	[dva'nadɛsɛt]
13 thirteen	тринадесет	[tri'nadɛsɛt]
14 fourteen	четиринадесет	[ʧɛtiri'nadɛsɛt]
15 fifteen	петнадесет	[pɛt'nadɛsɛt]
16 sixteen	шестнадесет	[ʃɛs'nadɛsɛt]
17 seventeen	седемнадесет	[sɛdɛm'nadɛsɛt]

| 18 eighteen | осемнадесет | [ɔsɛm'nadɛsɛt] |
| 19 nineteen | деветнадесет | [dɛvɛt'nadɛsɛt] |

20 twenty	двадесет	[d'vadɛsɛt]
30 thirty	тридесет	[t'ridɛsɛt]
40 forty	четиридесет	[tʃə'tiridɛsɛt]
50 fifty	петдесет	[pɛtdɛ'sɛt]

60 sixty	шестдесет	[ʃɛstdɛ'sɛt]
70 seventy	седемдесет	[sɛdɛmdɛ'sɛt]
80 eighty	осемдесет	[ɔsɛmdɛ'sɛt]
90 ninety	деветдесет	[dɛvɛtdɛ'sɛt]

100 one hundred	сто	[stɔ]
200 two hundred	двеста	[d'vɛsta]
300 three hundred	триста	[t'rista]
400 four hundred	четиристотин	['tʃətiris'totin]
500 five hundred	петстотин	['pɛts'totin]

600 six hundred	шестстотин	['ʃɛsts'totin]
700 seven hundred	седемстотин	['sɛdɛms'totin]
800 eight hundred	осемстотин	['ɔsɛms'totin]
900 nine hundred	деветстотин	['dɛvɛts'totin]
1000 one thousand	хиляда (ж)	[hi'ʎada]

| 10000 ten thousand | десет хиляди | ['dɛsɛt 'hiʎadi] |
| one hundred thousand | сто хиляди | [stɔ 'hiʎadi] |

| million | милион (м) | [mili'ɔn] |
| billion | милиард (м) | [mili'ard] |

3. Humans. Family

man (adult male)	мъж (м)	[mɪʒ]
young man	младеж (м)	[mla'dɛʒ]
teenager	тийнейджър (м)	[ti'nɛjdʒɪr]
woman	жена (ж)	[ʒɛ'na]
girl (young woman)	девойка (ж)	[dɛ'vɔjka]

age	възраст (ж)	['vɪzrast]
adult (adj)	възрастен	['vɪzrastɛn]
middle-aged (adj)	на средна възраст	[na s'rɛdna 'vɪzrast]
elderly (adj)	възрастен	['vɪzrastɛn]
old (adj)	стар	[star]

old man	старец (м)	[s'tarɛts]
old woman	старица (ж)	[s'taritsa]
retirement	пенсия (ж)	['pɛnsija]
to retire (from job)	пенсионирам се	[pɛnsio'niram sɛ]
retiree	пенсионер (м)	[pɛnsio'nɛr]

mother	майка (ж)	['majka]
father	баща (м)	[baʃta]
son	син (м)	[sin]
daughter	дъщеря (ж)	[dɪʃtɛ'rʲa]
brother	брат (м)	[brat]
sister	сестра (ж)	[sɛst'ra]

parents	родители (м мн)	[rɔ'ditɛli]
child	дете (с)	[dɛ'tɛ]
children	деца (с мн)	[dɛ'tsa]
stepmother	мащеха (ж)	['maʃtɛha]
stepfather	пастрок (м)	['pastrɔk]

grandmother	баба (ж)	['baba]
grandfather	дядо (м)	['dʲadɔ]
grandson	внук (м)	[vnuk]
granddaughter	внучка (ж)	[v'nutʃka]
grandchildren	внуци (м мн)	[v'nutsi]

uncle	вуйчо (м)	['vujtʃɔ]
aunt	леля (ж)	['lɛʎa]
nephew	племенник (м)	[p'lɛmɛnik]
niece	племенница (ж)	[p'lɛmɛnitsa]

wife	жена (ж)	[ʒɛ'na]
husband	мъж (м)	[mɪʒ]
married (masc.)	женен	['ʒɛnɛn]
married (fem.)	омъжена	[ɔ'mɪʒɛna]
widow	вдовица (ж)	[vdɔ'vitsa]
widower	вдовец (м)	[vdɔ'vɛts]

| name (first name) | име (с) | ['imɛ] |
| surname (last name) | фамилия (ж) | [fa'milija] |

relative	роднина (м, ж)	[rɔd'nina]
friend (masc.)	приятел (м)	[pri'jatɛl]
friendship	приятелство (с)	[pri'jatɛlstvɔ]

partner	партньор (м)	[part'nɔr]
superior (n)	началник (м)	[na'tʃalnik]
colleague	колега (м, ж)	[kɔ'lɛga]
neighbors	съседи (м мн)	[sɪ'sɛdi]

4. Human body

organism (body)	организъм (м)	[ɔrga'nizɪm]
body	тяло (с)	['tʲalɔ]
heart	сърце (с)	[sɪr'tsə]
blood	кръв (ж)	[krɪv]
brain	мозък (м)	['mɔzɪk]

nerve	нерв (м)	[nɛrv]
bone	кост (ж)	[kɔst]
skeleton	скелет (м)	[s'kɛlɛt]
spine (backbone)	гръбнак (м)	[grɪb'nak]
rib	ребро (с)	[rɛb'rɔ]
skull	череп (м)	['tʃərɛp]

muscle	мускул (м)	['muskul]
lungs	бели дробове (м мн)	['bɛli d'rɔbɔvɛ]
skin	кожа (ж)	['kɔʒa]

head	глава (ж)	[gla'va]
face	лице (с)	[li'tsə]
nose	нос (м)	[nɔs]
forehead	чело (с)	[tʃə'lɔ]
cheek	буза (ж)	['buza]

mouth	уста (ж)	[us'ta]
tongue	език (м)	[ɛ'zik]
tooth	зъб (м)	[zɪb]
lips	устни (ж мн)	['ustni]
chin	брадичка (ж)	[bra'ditʃka]

ear	ухо (с)	[u'hɔ]
neck	шия (ж)	['ʃija]
throat	гърло (с)	['gɪrlɔ]

eye	око (с)	[ɔ'kɔ]
pupil	зеница (ж)	['zɛnitsa]
eyebrow	вежда (ж)	['vɛʒda]
eyelash	мигла (ж)	['migla]

hair	коса (ж)	[kɔ'sa]
hairstyle	прическа (ж)	[pri'tʃəska]
mustache	мустаци (м мн)	[mus'tatsi]
beard	брада (ж)	[bra'da]
to have (a beard, etc.)	нося	['nɔsʲa]
bald (adj)	плешив	[plɛ'ʃiv]

hand	китка (ж)	['kitka]
arm	ръка (ж)	[rɪ'ka]
finger	пръст (м)	[prɪst]
nail	нокът (м)	['nɔkɪt]
palm	длан (ж)	[dlan]

shoulder	рамо (с)	['ramɔ]
leg	крак (м)	[krak]
foot	ходило (с)	[hɔ'dilɔ]
knee	коляно (с)	[kɔ'ʎanɔ]
heel	пета (ж)	[pɛ'ta]
back	гръб (м)	[grɪb]
waist	талия (ж)	['talija]

| beauty mark | бенка (ж) | ['bɛŋka] |
| birthmark (café au lait spot) | родилно петно (с) | [rɔ'dilnɔ pɛt'nɔ] |

5. Medicine. Diseases. Drugs

health	здраве (с)	[zd'ravɛ]
well (not sick)	здрав	[zdrav]
sickness	болест (ж)	['bɔlɛst]
to be sick	боледувам	[bɔlɛ'duvam]
ill, sick (adj)	болен	['bɔlɛn]

cold (illness)	настинка (ж)	[nas'tiŋka]
to catch a cold	настина	[nas'tina]
tonsillitis	ангина (ж)	[a'ŋgina]
pneumonia	възпаление (с) на белите дробове	[vɪspa'lɛniɛ na 'bɛlitɛ d'rɔbɔvɛ]
flu, influenza	грип (м)	[grip]

runny nose (coryza)	хрема (ж)	[h'rɛma]
cough	кашлица (ж)	['kaʃlitsa]
to cough (vi)	кашлям	['kaʃʎam]
to sneeze (vi)	кихам	['kiham]

stroke	инсулт (м)	[in'sult]
heart attack	инфаркт (м)	[in'farkt]
allergy	алергия (ж)	[a'lɛrgija]
asthma	астма (ж)	['astma]
diabetes	диабет (м)	[dia'bɛt]

tumor	тумор (м)	['tumɔr]
cancer	рак (м)	[rak]
alcoholism	алкохолизъм (м)	[alkɔhɔ'lizɪm]
AIDS	СПИН (м)	[spin]
fever	треска (ж)	[t'rɛska]
seasickness	морска болест (ж)	['mɔrska 'bɔlɛst]

bruise (hématome)	синина (ж)	[sini'na]
bump (lump)	подутина (ж)	[pɔduti'na]
to limp (vi)	куцам	['kutsam]
dislocation	изкълчване (с)	[is'kɪltʃvanɛ]
to dislocate (vt)	навехна	[na'vɛhna]

fracture	фрактура (ж)	[frak'tura]
burn (injury)	изгаряне (с)	[iz'garʲanɛ]
injury	рана (ж)	['rana]
pain	болка (ж)	['bɔlka]
toothache	зъбобол (м)	[zɪbɔ'bɔl]
to sweat (perspire)	потя се	[pɔ'tʲa sɛ]
deaf (adj)	глух	[gluh]

mute (adj)	ням	[ɲam]
immunity	имунитет (м)	[imuni'tɛt]
virus	вирус (м)	['virus]
microbe	микроб (м)	[mik'rɔb]
bacterium	бактерия (ж)	[bak'tɛrija]
infection	инфекция (ж)	[in'fɛktsija]
hospital	болница (ж)	['bɔlnitsa]
cure	лекуване (с)	[lɛ'kuvanɛ]
to vaccinate (vt)	ваксинирам	[vaksi'niram]
to be in a coma	намирам се в кома	[na'miram sɛ v 'kɔma]
intensive care	реанимация (ж)	[rɛani'matsija]
symptom	симптом (м)	[simp'tɔm]
pulse	пулс (м)	[puls]

6. Feelings. Emotions. Conversation

I, me	аз	[az]
you	ти	[ti]
he	той	[tɔj]
she	тя	[tʲa]
it	то	[tɔ]
we	ние	['niɛ]
you (to a group)	вие	['viɛ]
they	те	[tɛ]
Hello! (fam.)	Здравей!	[zdra'vɛj]
Hello! (form.)	Здравейте!	[zdra'vɛjtɛ]
Good morning!	Добро утро!	[dɔb'rɔ 'utrɔ]
Good afternoon!	Добър ден!	['dɔbɪr dɛn]
Good evening!	Добър вечер!	['dɔbɪr 'vɛtʃər]
to say hello	поздравявам	[pozdra'vʲavam]
to greet (vt)	приветствувам	[pri'vɛtstvuvam]
How are you?	Как си?	[kak si]
Bye-Bye! Goodbye!	Довиждане!	[dɔ'viʒdanɛ]
Thank you!	Благодаря!	[blagoda'rʲa]
feelings	чувства (с мн)	['tʃustva]
to be hungry	искам да ям	['iskam da jam]
to be thirsty	искам да пия	['iskam da 'pija]
tired (adj)	изморен	[izmɔ'rɛn]
to be worried	безпокоя се	[bɛspɔkɔ'ja sɛ]
to be nervous	нервирам се	[ner'viram sɛ]
hope	надежда (ж)	[na'dɛʒda]
to hope (vi, vt)	надявам се	[na'dʲavam sɛ]
character	характер (м)	[ha'raktɛr]
modest (adj)	скромен	[sk'rɔmɛn]

lazy (adj)	мързелив	[mɪrzɛ'liv]
generous (adj)	щедър	[ʃ'tɛdɪr]
talented (adj)	талантлив	[talant'lif]

honest (adj)	честен	['tʃəstɛn]
serious (adj)	сериозен	[sɛri'ɔzɛn]
shy, timid (adj)	свенлив	[svɛn'liv]
sincere (adj)	искрен	['iskrɛn]
coward	страхливец (м)	[strah'livɛts]

to sleep (vi)	спя	[spʲa]
dream	сън (м)	[sɪn]
bed	легло (с)	[lɛg'lɔ]
pillow	възглавница (ж)	[vɪzg'lavnitsa]

insomnia	безсъние (с)	[bɛs'sɪniɛ]
to go to bed	отивам да спя	[ɔ'tivam da spʲa]
nightmare	кошмар (м)	[kɔʃ'mar]
alarm clock	будилник (м)	[bu'dilnik]

smile	усмивка (ж)	[us'mifka]
to smile (vi)	усмихвам се	[us'mihvam sɛ]
to laugh (vi)	смея се	[s'mɛja sɛ]

quarrel	караница (ж)	['karanitsa]
insult	оскърбление (с)	[ɔskɪrb'lɛniɛ]
resentment	обида (ж)	[ɔ'bida]
angry (mad)	сърдит	[sɪr'dit]

7. Clothing. Personal accessories

clothes	облекло (с)	[ɔblɛk'lɔ]
coat (overcoat)	палто (с)	[pal'tɔ]
fur coat	кожено палто (с)	['kɔʒɛnɔ pal'tɔ]
jacket (e.g., leather ~)	яке (с)	['jakɛ]
raincoat (trenchcoat, etc.)	шлифер (м)	[ʃ'lifɛr]

shirt (button shirt)	риза (ж)	['riza]
pants	панталон (м)	[panta'lɔn]
suit jacket	сако (с)	[sa'kɔ]
suit	костюм (м)	[kɔs'tym]

dress (frock)	рокля (ж)	['rɔkʎa]
skirt	пола (ж)	[pɔ'la]
T-shirt	тениска (ж)	['tɛniska]
bathrobe	хавлиен халат (м)	[hav'lien ha'lat]
pajamas	пижама (ж)	[pi'ʒama]
workwear	работно облекло (с)	[ra'bɔtnɔ ɔblɛk'lɔ]
underwear	бельо (с)	[bɛ'lɔ]
socks	чорапи (м мн)	[tʃɔ'rapi]

bra	сутиен (м)	[suti'ɛn]
pantyhose	чорапогащник (м)	[ʧɔrapɔ'gaʃtnik]
stockings (thigh highs)	чорапи (м мн)	[ʧɔ'rapi]
bathing suit	бански (м)	['banski]

hat	шапка (ж)	['ʃʌpka]
footwear	обувки (ж мн)	[ɔ'bufki]
boots (cowboy ~)	ботуши (м мн)	[bɔ'tuʃi]
heel	ток (м)	[tɔk]
shoestring	връзка (ж)	[v'rɪska]
shoe polish	крем (м) за обувки	[krɛm za ɔ'buvki]

cotton (n)	памук (м)	[pa'muk]
wool (n)	вълна (ж)	['vɪlna]
fur (n)	кожа (ж)	['kɔʒa]

gloves	ръкавици (ж мн)	[rɪka'viʦi]
mittens	ръкавици (ж мн) с един пръст	[rɪka'viʦi s ɛ'din prɪst]
scarf (muffler)	шал (м)	[ʃʌl]
glasses (eyeglasses)	очила (мн)	[ɔʧi'la]
umbrella	чадър (м)	[ʧa'dɪr]

tie (necktie)	вратовръзка (ж)	[vratɔv'rɪzka]
handkerchief	носна кърпичка (ж)	['nɔsna 'kɪrpiʧka]
comb	гребен (м)	[g'rɛbɛn]
hairbrush	четка (ж) за коса	['ʧɘtka za kɔ'sa]

buckle	катарама (ж)	[kata'rama]
belt	колан (м)	[kɔ'lan]
purse	чантичка (ж)	['ʧantiʧka]

collar	яка (ж)	[jɑ'ka]
pocket	джоб (м)	[dʒɔb]
sleeve	ръкав (м)	[rɪ'kav]
fly (on trousers)	копчелък (м)	[kɔpʧɘ'lɪk]

zipper (fastener)	цип (м)	[ʦip]
button	копче (с)	['kɔpʧɘ]
to get dirty (vi)	изцапам се	[is'ʦapam sɛ]
stain (mark, spot)	петно (с)	[pɛt'nɔ]

8. City. Urban institutions

store	магазин (м)	[maga'zin]
shopping mall	търговски център (м)	[tɪr'gɔvski 'ʦɛntɪr]
supermarket	супермаркет (м)	[supɛr'markɛt]
shoe store	магазин (м) за обувки	[maga'zin za ɔ'bufki]
bookstore	книжарница (ж)	[kni'ʒarniʦa]
drugstore, pharmacy	аптека (ж)	[ap'tɛka]

bakery	хлебарница (ж)	[hlɛ'barnitsa]
candy store	сладкарница (ж)	[slad'karnitsa]
grocery store	бакалия (ж)	[baka'lija]
butcher shop	месарница (ж)	[mɛ'sarnitsa]
produce store	магазинче (с) за плодове и зеленчуци	[maga'zintʃə za plɔdɔ've i zɛlɛn'tʃutsi]
market	пазар (м)	[pa'zar]

hair salon	фризьорски салон (м)	[fri'zɜrski sa'lɔn]
post office	поща (ж)	['pɔʃta]
dry cleaners	химическо чистене (с)	[hi'mitʃɛskɔ 'tʃistɛnɛ]
circus	цирк (м)	[tsirk]
zoo	зоологическа градина (ж)	[zɔːlɔ'gitʃɛska gra'dina]

theater	театър (м)	[tɛ'atɪr]
movie theater	кино (с)	['kinɔ]
museum	музей (м)	[mu'zɛj]
library	библиотека (ж)	[biblio'tɛka]

mosque	джамия (ж)	[dʒa'mija]
synagogue	синагога (ж)	[sina'gɔga]
cathedral	катедрала (ж)	[katɛd'rala]
temple	храм (м)	[hram]
church	църква (ж)	['tsɪrkva]

college	институт (м)	[insti'tut]
university	университет (м)	[univɛrsi'tɛt]
school	училище (с)	[u'tʃiliʃtɛ]

hotel	хотел (м)	[hɔ'tɛl]
bank	банка (ж)	['baŋka]
embassy	посолство (с)	[pɔ'sɔlstvɔ]
travel agency	туристическа агенция (ж)	[turis'titʃɛska a'gɛntsija]

subway	метро (с)	[mɛt'rɔ]
hospital	болница (ж)	['bɔlnitsa]
gas station	бензиностанция (ж)	[bɛnzinɔs'tantsija]
parking lot	паркинг (м)	['parkiŋg]

ENTRANCE	ВХОД	[vhɔt]
EXIT	ИЗХОД	['ishɔt]
PUSH	БУТНИ	[but'ni]
PULL	ДРЪПНИ	[drɪp'ni]
OPEN	ОТВОРЕНО	[ɔt'vɔrɛnɔ]
CLOSED	ЗАТВОРЕНО	[zat'vɔrɛnɔ]

monument	паметник (м)	['pamɛtnik]
fortress	крепост (ж)	[k'rɛpɔst]
palace	дворец (м)	[dvɔ'rɛts]
medieval (adj)	средновековен	[srɛdnɔvɛ'kɔvɛn]

ancient (adj)	старинен	[sta'rinɛn]
national (adj)	национален	[natsiɔ'nalɛn]
well-known (adj)	известен	[iz'vɛstɛn]

9. Money. Finances

money	пари (мн)	[pa'ri]
coin	монета (ж)	[mɔ'nɛta]
dollar	долар (м)	['dɔlar]
euro	евро (с)	['ɛvrɔ]

ATM	банкомат (м)	[baŋkɔ'mat]
currency exchange	обменно бюро (с)	[ɔb'mɛŋɔ 'byrɔ]
exchange rate	курс (м)	[kurs]
cash	налични пари (мн)	[na'litʃni pa'ri]

How much?	Колко?	['kɔlkɔ]
to pay (vi, vt)	плащам	[p'laʃtam]
payment	плащане (с)	[p'laʃtanɛ]
change (give the ~)	ресто (с)	['rɛstɔ]

price	цена (ж)	[ʦə'na]
discount	намаление (с)	[nama'lɛniɛ]
cheap (adj)	евтин	['ɛftin]
expensive (adj)	скъп	[skɪp]

bank	банка (ж)	['baŋka]
account	сметка (ж)	[s'mɛtka]
credit card	кредитна карта (ж)	[k'rɛditna 'karta]
check	чек (м)	[tʃek]
to write a check	подпиша чек	[pɔt'piʃʌ tʃək]
checkbook	чекова книжка (ж)	['tʃəkɔva k'niʃka]

debt	дълг (м)	[dɪlg]
debtor	длъжник (м)	[dlɪʒ'nik]
to lend (money)	давам на заем	['davam na 'zaɛm]
to borrow (vi, vt)	взема на заем	[v'zɛma na 'zaɛm]

to rent (~ a tuxedo)	взимам под наем	[v'zimam pɔd 'naɛm]
on credit (adv)	на кредит	[na k'rɛdit]
wallet	портфейл (м)	[pɔrt'fɛjl]
safe	сейф (м)	[sɛjf]
inheritance	наследство (с)	[nas'lɛdstvɔ]
fortune (wealth)	състояние (с)	[sɪstɔ'jɑniɛ]

tax	данък (м)	['danɪk]
fine	глоба (ж)	[g'lɔba]
to fine (vt)	глобявам	[glɔ'bʲavam]
wholesale (adj)	на едро	[na 'ɛdrɔ]
retail (adj)	на дребно	[na d'rɛbnɔ]

to insure (vt)	застраховам	[zastra'hɔvam]
insurance	застраховка (ж)	[zastra'hɔfka]
capital	капитал (м)	[kapi'tal]
turnover	оборот (м)	[ɔbɔ'rɔt]
stock (share)	акция (ж)	['aktsija]
profit	печалба (ж)	[pɛ'tʃalba]
profitable (adj)	печеливш	[pɛtʃə'livʃ]
crisis	криза (ж)	[k'riza]
bankruptcy	фалит (м)	[fa'lit]
to go bankrupt	фалирам	[fa'liram]
accountant	счетоводител (м)	[stʃətɔvɔ'ditɛl]
salary	работна заплата (ж)	[ra'bɔtna zap'lata]
bonus (money)	премия (ж)	[p'rɛmija]

10. Transportation

bus	автобус (м)	[avtɔ'bus]
streetcar	трамвай (м)	[tram'vaj]
trolley bus	тролей (м)	[trɔ'lɛj]
to go by …	пътувам с …	[pɪ'tuvam s]
to get on (~ the bus)	качвам се в …	['katʃvam sɛ v]
to get off …	сляза от …	[s'ʎaza ɔt]
stop (e.g., bus ~)	спирка (ж)	[s'pirka]
terminus	последна спирка (ж)	[pɔs'lɛdna s'pirka]
schedule	разписание (с)	[raspi'saniɛ]
ticket	билет (м)	[bi'lɛt]
to be late (for …)	закъснявам	[zakɪs'ɲavam]
taxi, cab	такси (с)	[tak'si]
by taxi	с такси	[s tak'si]
taxi stand	пиаца (ж) на такси	[pi'atsa na tak'si]
traffic	улично движение (с)	['ulitʃnɔ dvi'ʒɛniɛ]
rush hour	час пик (м)	[tʃas 'pik]
to park (vi)	паркирам се	[par'kiram sɛ]
subway	метро (с)	[mɛt'rɔ]
station	станция (ж)	[s'tantsija]
train	влак (м)	[vlak]
train station	гара (ж)	['gara]
rails	релси (ж мн)	['rɛlsi]
compartment	купе (с)	[ku'pɛ]
berth	легло (с)	[lɛg'lɔ]
airplane	самолет (м)	[samɔ'lɛt]
air ticket	самолетен билет (м)	[samɔ'lɛtɛn bi'lɛt]

airline	авиокомпания (ж)	[aviokɔm'panija]
airport	летище (с)	[lɛ'tiʃtɛ]
flight (act of flying)	полет (м)	['pɔlɛt]
luggage	багаж (м)	[ba'gaʃ]
luggage cart	количка (ж)	[kɔ'litʃka]
ship	кораб (м)	['kɔrab]
cruise ship	рейсов кораб (м)	['rɛjsɔv 'kɔrab]
yacht	яхта (ж)	['jahta]
boat (flat-bottomed ~)	лодка (ж)	['lɔtka]
captain	капитан (м)	[kapi'tan]
cabin	каюта (ж)	[ka'juta]
port (harbor)	пристанище (с)	[pris'taniʃtɛ]
bicycle	колело (с)	[kɔlɛ'lɔ]
scooter	моторолер (м)	['mɔtɔ'rɔler]
motorcycle, bike	мотоциклет (м)	[mɔtɔtsik'lɛt]
pedal	педал (м)	[pɛ'dal]
pump	помпа (ж)	['pɔmpa]
wheel	колело (с)	[kɔlɛ'lɔ]
automobile, car	автомобил (м)	[avtɔmɔ'bil]
ambulance	бърза помощ (ж)	['bɪrza 'pɔmɔʃt]
truck	камион (м)	[kami'ɔn]
used (adj)	употребяван	[upɔtrɛ'bʲavan]
car crash	катастрофа (ж)	[katast'rɔfa]
repair	ремонт (м)	[rɛ'mɔnt]

11. Food. Part 1

meat	месо (с)	[mɛ'sɔ]
chicken	кокошка (ж)	[kɔ'kɔʃka]
duck	патица (ж)	['patitsa]
pork	свинско (с)	[s'vinskɔ]
veal	телешко месо (с)	['tɛlɛʃkɔ me'sɔ]
lamb	агнешко (с)	['agnɛʃkɔ]
beef	говеждо (с)	[gɔ'vɛʒdɔ]
sausage (bologna, pepperoni, etc.)	салам (м)	[sa'lam]
egg	яйце (с)	[jɑj'tsə]
fish	риба (ж)	['riba]
cheese	кашкавал (м)	[kaʃka'val]
sugar	захар (ж)	['zahar]
salt	сол (ж)	[sɔl]
rice	ориз (м)	[ɔ'riz]
pasta	макарони (мн)	[maka'rɔni]

butter	краве масло (c)	[k'ravɛ mas'lɔ]
vegetable oil	олио (c)	['ɔliɔ]
bread	хляб (м)	[hʎab]
chocolate (n)	шоколад (м)	[ʃɔkɔ'lad]

wine	вино (c)	['vinɔ]
coffee	кафе (c)	[ka'fɛ]
milk	мляко (c)	[m'ʎakɔ]
juice	сок (м)	[sɔk]
beer	бира (ж)	['bira]
tea	чай (м)	[ʧaj]

tomato	домат (м)	[dɔ'mat]
cucumber	краставица (ж)	[k'rastaviʦa]
carrot	морков (м)	['mɔrkɔf]
potato	картофи (мн)	[kar'tɔfi]
onion	лук (м)	[luk]
garlic	чесън (м)	['ʧəsɪn]

cabbage	зеле (c)	['zɛlɛ]
beetroot	цвекло (c)	[ʦvɛk'lɔ]
eggplant	патладжан (м)	[patla'dʒan]
dill	копър (м)	['kɔpɪr]
lettuce	салата (ж)	[sa'lata]
corn (maize)	царевица (ж)	['ʦarɛviʦa]

fruit	плод (м)	[plɔt]
apple	ябълка (ж)	['jɑbɪlka]
pear	круша (ж)	[k'ruʃʌ]
lemon	лимон (м)	[li'mɔn]
orange	портокал (м)	[pɔrtɔ'kal]
strawberry	ягода (ж)	['jɑgɔda]

plum	слива (ж)	[s'liva]
raspberry	малина (ж)	[ma'lina]
pineapple	ананас (м)	[ana'nas]
banana	банан (м)	[ba'nan]
watermelon	диня (ж)	['diɲa]
grape	грозде (c)	[g'rɔzdɛ]
melon	пъпеш (м)	['pɪpɛʃ]

12. Food. Part 2

cuisine	кухня (ж)	['kuhɲa]
recipe	рецепта (ж)	[rɛ'ʦəpta]
food	храна (ж)	[hra'na]

to have breakfast	закусвам	[za'kusvam]
to have lunch	обядвам	[ɔ'bʲadvam]
to have dinner	вечерям	[vɛ'ʧərʲam]

taste, flavor	вкус (м)	[vkus]
tasty (adj)	вкусен	[v'kusɛn]
cold (adj)	студен	[stu'dɛn]
hot (adj)	горещ	[gɔ'rɛʃt]
sweet (sugary)	сладък	[s'ladık]
salty (adj)	солен	[sɔ'lɛn]

sandwich (bread)	сандвич (м)	['sandvitʃ]
side dish	гарнитура (ж)	[garni'tura]
filling (for cake, pie)	плънка (ж)	[p'lıŋka]
sauce	сос (м)	[sɔs]
piece (of cake, pie)	парче (с)	[par'tʃə]

diet	диета (ж)	[di'ɛta]
vitamin	витамин (м)	[vita'min]
calorie	калория (ж)	[ka'lɔrija]
vegetarian (n)	вегетарианец (м)	[vɛgɛtari'anɛts]

restaurant	ресторант (м)	[rɛstɔ'rant]
coffee house	кафене (с)	[kafɛ'nɛ]
appetite	апетит (м)	[apɛ'tit]
Enjoy your meal!	Добър апетит!	[dɔ'bır apɛ'tit]

waiter	сервитьор (м)	[sɛrvi'tɜr]
waitress	сервитьорка (ж)	[sɛrvi'tɜrka]
bartender	барман (м)	['barman]
menu	меню (с)	[mɛ'ny]

spoon	лъжица (ж)	[lı'ʒitsa]
knife	нож (м)	[nɔʒ]
fork	вилица (ж)	['vilitsa]
cup (e.g., coffee ~)	чаша (ж)	['tʃaʃʌ]

plate (dinner ~)	чиния (ж)	[tʃi'nija]
saucer	чинийка (ж)	[tʃi'nijka]
napkin (on table)	салфетка (ж)	[sal'fɛtka]
toothpick	клечка (ж) за зъби	[k'lɛtʃka za 'zıbi]

to order (meal)	поръчам	[pɔ'rıtʃam]
course, dish	ястие (с)	['jastiɛ]
portion	порция (ж)	['pɔrtsija]
appetizer	мезе (с)	[mɛ'zɛ]
salad	салата (ж)	[sa'lata]
soup	супа (ж)	['supa]

dessert	десерт (м)	[dɛ'sɛrt]
whole fruit jam	сладко (с)	[s'ladkɔ]
ice-cream	сладолед (м)	[sladɔ'lɛd]

check	сметка (ж)	[s'mɛtka]
to pay the check	плащам сметка	[p'laʃtam s'mɛtka]
tip	бакшиш (м)	[bak'ʃiʃ]

13. House. Apartment. Part 1

house	къща (ж)	['kɪʃta]
country house	извънградска къща (ж)	[izvɪŋg'ratska 'kɪʃta]
villa (seaside ~)	вила (ж)	['vila]
floor, story	етаж (м)	[ɛ'taʒ]
entrance	вход (м)	[vhɔd]
wall	стена (ж)	[stɛ'na]
roof	покрив (м)	['pɔkriv]
chimney	тръба (ж)	[trɪ'ba]
attic (storage place)	таван (м)	[ta'van]
window	прозорец (м)	[prɔ'zɔrɛts]
window ledge	перваз (м) за прозорец	[pɛr'vas za prɔ'zɔrɛts]
balcony	балкон (м)	[bal'kɔn]
stairs (stairway)	стълба (ж)	[s'tɪlba]
mailbox	пощенска кутия (ж)	['pɔʃtɛnska ku'tijɑ]
garbage can	контейнер (м) за отпадъци	[kɔn'tɛjnɛr za ɔt'padɪtsi]
elevator	асансьор (м)	[asan'sɜr]
electricity	електричество (с)	[ɛlɛkt'ritʃəstvɔ]
light bulb	крушка (ж)	[k'ruʃka]
switch	изключвател (м)	[izklytʃ'vatɛl]
wall socket	контакт (м)	[kɔn'takt]
fuse	предпазител (м)	[prɛd'pazitɛl]
door	врата (ж)	[vra'ta]
handle, doorknob	дръжка (ж)	[d'rɪʃka]
key	ключ (м)	[klytʃ]
doormat	килимче (с)	[ki'limtʃə]
door lock	брава (ж)	[b'rava]
doorbell	звънец (м)	[zvɪ'nɛts]
knock (at the door)	чукане (с)	['tʃukanɛ]
to knock (vi)	чукам	['tʃukam]
peephole	шпионка (ж)	[ʃpi'ɔŋka]
yard	двор (м)	[dvɔr]
garden	градина (ж)	[gra'dina]
swimming pool	басейн (м)	[ba'sɛjn]
gym (home gym)	спортна зала (ж)	[s'pɔrtna 'zala]
tennis court	тенис корт (м)	['tɛnis kɔrt]
garage	гараж (м)	[ga'raʒ]
private property	частна собственост (ж)	['tʃasna 'sɔpstvɛnɔst]
warning sign	предупредителен надпис (м)	[prɛduprɛ'ditɛlɛn 'natpis]
security	охрана (ж)	[ɔh'rana]

security guard	охранител (м)	[ɔhra'nitɛl]
renovations	ремонт (м)	[rɛ'mɔnt]
to renovate (vt)	правя ремонт	[p'ravʲa rɛ'mɔnt]
to put in order	подреждам	[pɔd'rɛʒdam]
to paint (~ a wall)	боядисвам	[bɔja'disvam]
wallpaper	тапети (м мн)	[ta'pɛti]
to varnish (vt)	лакирам	[la'kiram]
pipe	тръба (ж)	[trɪ'ba]
tools	инструменти (м мн)	[instru'mɛnti]
basement	мазе (с)	[ma'zɛ]
sewerage (system)	канализация (ж)	[kanali'zaʦija]

14. House. Apartment. Part 2

apartment	апартамент (м)	[aparta'mɛnt]
room	стая (ж)	[s'taja]
bedroom	спалня (ж)	[s'palɲa]
dining room	столова (ж)	[stɔlɔ'va]
living room	гостна (ж)	['gɔstna]
study (home office)	кабинет (м)	[kabi'nɛt]
entry room	антре (с)	[ant'rɛ]
bathroom (room with a bath or shower)	баня (ж)	['baɲa]
half bath	тоалетна (ж)	[tɔa'lɛtna]
floor	под (м)	[pɔd]
ceiling	таван (м)	[ta'van]
to dust (vt)	изтривам прах	[ist'rivam prah]
vacuum cleaner	прахосмукачка (ж)	[prahɔsmu'kaʧka]
to vacuum (vt)	почиствам с прахосмукачка	[pɔ'ʧistvam s prahɔsmu'kaʧka]
mop	четка (ж) за под	['ʧətka za pɔd]
dust cloth	парцал (м)	[par'ʦal]
short broom	метла (ж)	[mɛt'la]
dustpan	лопатка (ж) за боклук	[lɔ'patka za bɔk'luk]
furniture	мебели (мн)	['mɛbɛli]
table	маса (ж)	['masa]
chair	стол (м)	[stɔl]
armchair	фотьойл (м)	[fɔ'tɔjl]
bookcase	книжен шкаф (м)	[k'niʒɛn ʃkaf]
shelf	рафт (м)	[raft]
wardrobe	гардероб (м)	[gardɛ'rɔb]
mirror	огледало (с)	[ɔglɛ'dalɔ]
carpet	килим (м)	[ki'lim]

fireplace	камина (ж)	[ka'mina]
drapes	пердета (с мн)	[pɛr'dɛta]
table lamp	лампа (ж) за маса	['lampa za 'masa]
chandelier	полилей (м)	[pɔli'lɛj]

kitchen	кухня (ж)	['kuhɲa]
gas stove (range)	газова печка (ж)	['gazɔva 'pɛtʃka]
electric stove	електрическа печка (ж)	[ɛlɛkt'ritʃeska 'pɛtʃka]
microwave oven	микровълнова печка (ж)	[mikrɔ'vɪlnɔva 'pɛtʃka]

refrigerator	хладилник (м)	[hla'dilnik]
freezer	фризер (м)	[f'rizɛr]
dishwasher	съдомиялна машина (ж)	[sɪdɔmi'jalna ma'ʃina]
faucet	смесител (м)	[smɛ'sitɛl]

meat grinder	месомелачка (ж)	[mɛsɔmɛ'latʃka]
juicer	сокоизстисквачка (ж)	[sɔkɔizstisk'vatʃka]
toaster	тостер (м)	['tɔstɛr]
mixer	миксер (м)	['miksɛr]

coffee machine	кафеварка (ж)	[kafɛ'varka]
kettle	чайник (м)	['tʃajnik]
teapot	чайник (м)	['tʃajnik]

TV set	телевизор (м)	[tɛlɛ'vizɔr]
VCR (video recorder)	видео (с)	['vidɛɔ]
iron (e.g., steam ~)	ютия (ж)	[ju'tija]
telephone	телефон (м)	[tɛlɛ'fɔn]

15. Professions. Social status

director	директор (м)	[di'rɛktɔr]
superior	началник (м)	[na'tʃalnik]
president	президент (м)	[prɛzi'dɛnt]
assistant	помощник (м)	[pɔ'mɔʃtnik]
secretary	секретар (м)	[sɛkrɛ'tar]

owner, proprietor	собственик (м)	['sɔbstvɛnik]
partner	партньор (м)	[part'nɜr]
stockholder	акционер (м)	[aktsiɔ'nɛr]

businessman	бизнесмен (м)	[biznɛs'mɛn]
millionaire	милионер (м)	[miliɔ'nɛr]
billionaire	милиардер (м)	[miliar'dɛr]

actor	актьор (м)	[ak'tɜr]
architect	архитект (м)	[arhi'tɛkt]
banker	банкер (м)	[ba'ŋkɛr]
broker	брокер (м)	[b'rɔkɛr]
veterinarian	ветеринар (м)	[vɛtɛri'nar]

doctor	лекар (м)	['lɛkar]
chambermaid	камериерка (ж)	[kamɛri'ɛrka]
designer	дизайнер (м)	[di'zajnɛr]
correspondent	кореспондент (м)	[kɔrɛspɔn'dɛnt]
delivery man	куриер (м)	[kuri'ɛr]

electrician	монтьор (м)	[mɔn'tɜr]
musician	музикант (м)	[muzi'kant]
babysitter	детегледачка (ж)	[dɛtɛglɛ'datʃka]
hairdresser	фризьор (м)	[fri'zʲɔr]
herder, shepherd	пастир (м)	[pas'tir]

singer (masc.)	певец (м)	[pɛ'vɛʦ]
translator	преводач (м)	[prɛvɔ'datʃ]
writer	писател (м)	[pi'satɛl]
carpenter	дърводелец (м)	[dɪrvɔ'dɛlɛʦ]
cook	готвач (м)	[gɔt'vatʃ]

fireman	пожарникар (м)	[pɔʒarni'kar]
police officer	полицай (м)	[pɔli'ʦaj]
mailman	пощальон (м)	[pɔʃta'lʲɔn]
programmer	програмист (м)	[prɔgra'mist]
salesman (store staff)	продавач (м)	[prɔda'vatʃ]

worker	работник (м)	[ra'bɔtnik]
gardener	градинар (м)	[gradi'nar]
plumber	водопроводчик (м)	[vɔdɔprɔ'vɔdtʃik]
dentist	стоматолог (м)	[stɔmatɔ'lɔg]
flight attendant (fem.)	стюардеса (ж)	[styar'dɛsa]

dancer (masc.)	танцьор (м)	[tan'ʦɜr]
bodyguard	телохранител (с)	[tɛlɔhra'nitɛl]
scientist	учен (м)	['utʃən]
schoolteacher	учител (м)	[u'tʃitɛl]

farmer	фермер (м)	['fɛrmɛr]
surgeon	хирург (м)	[hi'rurg]
miner	миньор (м)	[mi'nɜr]
chef (kitchen chef)	главен готвач (м)	[g'lavɛn gɔt'vatʃ]
driver	шофьор (м)	[ʃɔ'fɜr]

16. Sport

kind of sports	вид (м) спорт	[vid spɔrt]
soccer	футбол (м)	['fudbɔl]
hockey	хокей (м)	['hɔkɛj]
basketball	баскетбол (м)	['baskɛtbɔl]
baseball	бейзбол (м)	[bɛjz'bɔl]
volleyball	волейбол (м)	['vɔlɛjbɔl]
boxing	бокс (м)	[bɔks]

wrestling	борба (ж)	[bɔr'ba]
tennis	тенис (м)	['tɛnis]
swimming	плуване (с)	[p'luvanɛ]

chess	шахмат (м)	['ʃʌh'mat]
running	бягане (с)	['bʲaganɛ]
athletics	лека атлетика (ж)	['lɛka at'lɛtika]
figure skating	фигурно пързаляне (с)	['figurnɔ pɪr'zaʎanɛ]
cycling	колоездене (с)	[kɔlɔ'ɛzdɛnɛ]

billiards	билярд (м)	[bi'ʎard]
bodybuilding	културизъм (м)	[kultu'rizɪm]
golf	голф (м)	[gɔlf]
scuba diving	дайвинг (м)	['dajviŋg]
sailing	спорт (м) с платноходки	[spɔrt s platnɔ'hɔtki]

period, half	полувреме (с)	[pɔluv'rɛmɛ]
half-time	почивка (ж)	[pɔ'tʃifka]
tie	наравно	[na'ravnɔ]
to tie (vi)	завърша наравно	[za'vɪrʃʌ na'ravnɔ]

treadmill	писта за бягане (ж)	['pista za 'bʲaganɛ]
player	играч (м)	[ig'ratʃ]
substitute	резервен играч (м)	[rɛ'zɛrvɛn ig'ratʃ]
substitutes bench	резервна скамейка (ж)	[rɛ'zɛrvna ska'mɛjka]

match	мач (м)	[matʃ]
goal	врата (ж)	[vra'ta]
goalkeeper	вратар (м)	[vra'tar]
goal (score)	гол (м)	[gɔl]

Olympic Games	олимпийски игри (ж мн)	[ɔlim'pijski ig'ri]
to set a record	поставям рекорд	[pɔs'tavʲam rɛ'kɔrd]
final	финал (м)	[fi'nal]
champion	шампион (м)	[ʃʌm'piɔn]
championship	шампионат (м)	[ʃʌmpiɔ'nat]

winner	победител (м)	[pɔbɛ'ditɛl]
victory	победа (ж)	[pɔ'bɛda]
to win (vi)	спечеля	[spɛ'tʃəʎa]

| to lose (not win) | загубя | [za'gubʲa] |
| medal | медал (м) | [mɛ'dal] |

first place	първо място (с)	['pɪrvɔ 'mʲastɔ]
second place	второ място (с)	[f'tɔrɔ 'mʲastɔ]
third place	трето място (с)	[t'rɛtɔ 'mʲastɔ]

stadium	стадион (м)	[stadi'ɔn]
fan, supporter	запалянко (м)	[zapa'ʎaŋkɔ]
trainer, coach	треньор (м)	[trɛ'nɔr]
training	тренировка (ж)	[trɛni'rɔfka]

17. Foreign languages. Orthography

language	език (m)	[ɛ'zik]
to study (vt)	изучавам	[izu'tʃavam]
pronunciation	произношение (c)	[prɔiznɔ'ʃɛniɛ]
accent	акцент (m)	[ak'tsənt]
noun	съществително име (c)	[sɪʃtɛst'vitɛlnɔ 'imɛ]
adjective	прилагателно име (c)	[prila'gatɛlnɔ 'imɛ]
verb	глагол (m)	[gla'gɔl]
adverb	наречие (c)	[na'rɛtʃiɛ]
pronoun	местоимение (c)	[mɛstɔi'mɛniɛ]
interjection	междуметие (c)	[mɛʒdu'mɛtiɛ]
preposition	предлог (m)	[prɛd'lɔg]
root	корен (m) на думата	['kɔrɛn na 'dumata]
ending	окончание (c)	[ɔkɔn'tʃaniɛ]
prefix	представка (ж)	[prɛts'tafka]
syllable	сричка (ж)	[s'ritʃka]
suffix	наставка (ж)	[nas'tafka]
stress mark	ударение (c)	[uda'rɛniɛ]
period, dot	точка (ж)	['tɔtʃka]
comma	запетая (ж)	[zapɛ'tajɑ]
colon	двоеточие (c)	[dvɔɛ'tɔtʃiɛ]
ellipsis	многоточие (c)	[mnɔgɔ'tɔtʃiɛ]
question	въпрос (m)	[vɪp'rɔs]
question mark	въпросителен знак (m)	[vɪprɔ'sitɛlen z'nak]
exclamation point	удивителна (ж)	[udi'vitɛlna]
in quotation marks	в кавички	[v ka'vitʃki]
in parenthesis	в скоби	[v s'kɔbi]
letter	буква (ж)	['bukva]
capital letter	главна буква (ж)	[g'lavna 'bukva]
sentence	изречение (c)	[izrɛ'tʃɛniɛ]
group of words	словосъчетание (c)	[slɔvɔsɪtʃə'taniɛ]
expression	израз (m)	['izraz]
subject	подлог (m)	['pɔdlɔg]
predicate	сказуемо (c)	[ska'zuɛmɔ]
line	ред (m)	[rɛd]
paragraph	абзац (m)	[ab'zats]
synonym	синоним (m)	[sinɔ'nim]
antonym	антоним (m)	[antɔ'nim]
exception	изключение (c)	[izkly'tʃəniɛ]
to underline (vt)	подчертая	[pɔdtʃər'tajɑ]
rules	правила (c мн)	[pravi'la]

grammar	граматика (ж)	[gra'matika]
vocabulary	лексика (ж)	['lɛksika]
phonetics	фонетика (ж)	[fo'nɛtika]
alphabet	алфавит (м)	[alfa'vit]

textbook	учебник (м)	[u'ʧəbnik]
dictionary	речник (м)	['rɛʧnik]
phrasebook	разговорник (м)	[razgo'vɔrnik]

word	дума (ж)	['duma]
meaning	смисъл (м)	[s'misıl]
memory	памет (ж)	['pamɛt]

18. The Earth. Geography

the Earth	Земя	[zɛ'mʲa]
the globe (the Earth)	земно кълбо (с)	['zɛmnɔ kıl'bɔ]
planet	планета (ж)	[pla'nɛta]

geography	география (ж)	[gɛɔg'rafijɑ]
nature	природа (ж)	[pri'rɔda]
map	карта (ж)	['karta]
atlas	атлас (м)	[at'las]

in the north	на север	[na 'sɛvɛr]
in the south	на юг	[na jug]
in the west	на запад	[na 'zapat]
in the east	на изток	[na 'istɔk]

sea	море (с)	[mɔ'rɛ]
ocean	океан (м)	[ɔkɛ'an]
gulf (bay)	залив (м)	['zalif]
straits	пролив (м)	[p'rɔliv]

continent (mainland)	материк (м)	[matɛ'rik]
island	остров (м)	['ɔstrɔv]
peninsula	полуостров (м)	[pɔlu'ɔstrɔv]
archipelago	архипелаг (м)	[arhipɛ'lag]

harbor	залив (м)	['zalif]
coral reef	коралов риф (м)	[kɔ'ralɔv rif]
shore	бряг (м)	[brʲag]
coast	крайбрежие (с)	[krajb'rɛʒiɛ]

| flow (flood tide) | прилив (м) | [p'riliv] |
| ebb (ebb tide) | отлив (м) | ['ɔtliv] |

latitude	ширина (ж)	[ʃiri'na]
longitude	дължина (ж)	[dıʒi'na]
parallel	паралел (ж)	[para'lɛl]

equator	**екватор** (м)	[ɛk'vatɔr]
sky	**небе** (с)	[nɛ'bɛ]
horizon	**хоризонт** (м)	[hɔri'zɔnt]
atmosphere	**атмосфера** (ж)	[atmɔs'fɛra]

mountain	**планина** (ж)	[plani'na]
summit, top	**връх** (м)	[vrɪh]
cliff	**скала** (ж)	[ska'la]
hill	**хълм** (м)	[hɪlm]

volcano	**вулкан** (м)	[vul'kan]
glacier	**ледник** (м)	['lɛdnik]
waterfall	**водопад** (м)	[vɔdɔ'pad]
plain	**равнина** (ж)	[ravni'na]

river	**река** (ж)	[rɛ'ka]
spring (natural source)	**извор** (м)	['izvɔr]
bank (of river)	**бряг** (м)	[brʲag]
downstream (adv)	**надолу по течението**	[na'dɔlu pɔ tɛ'tʃɛniɛtɔ]
upstream (adv)	**нагоре по течението**	[na'gɔrɛ pɔ tɛ'tʃɛniɛtɔ]

lake	**езеро** (с)	['ɛzɛrɔ]
dam	**яз** (м)	[jɑz]
canal	**канал** (м)	[ka'nal]
swamp (marshland)	**блато** (с)	[b'latɔ]
ice	**лед** (м)	[lɛd]

19. Countries of the world. Part 1

Europe	**Европа**	[ɛv'rɔpa]
European Union	**Европейски Съюз** (м)	[ɛvrɔ'pɛjski sɪ'juz]
European (n)	**европеец** (м)	[ɛvrɔ'pɛːts]
European (adj)	**европейски**	[ɛvrɔ'pɛjski]

Austria	**Австрия**	['afstrijɑ]
Great Britain	**Великобритания**	[vɛlikɔbri'tanijɑ]
England	**Англия**	['aŋglijɑ]
Belgium	**Белгия**	['bɛlgijɑ]
Germany	**Германия**	[gɛr'manijɑ]

Netherlands	**Нидерландия**	[nidɛr'landijɑ]
Holland	**Холандия** (ж)	[hɔ'landijɑ]
Greece	**Гърция**	['gɪrtsijɑ]
Denmark	**Дания**	['danijɑ]
Ireland	**Ирландия**	[ir'landijɑ]

Iceland	**Исландия**	[is'landijɑ]
Spain	**Испания**	[is'panijɑ]
Italy	**Италия**	[i'talijɑ]
Cyprus	**Кипър**	['kipɪr]

Malta	Малта	['malta]
Norway	Норвегия	[nɔr'vɛgija]
Portugal	Португалия	[pɔrtu'galija]
Finland	Финландия	[fin'landija]
France	Франция	[f'rantsija]
Sweden	Швеция	[ʃ'vɛtsija]

Switzerland	Швейцария	[ʃvɛj'tsarija]
Scotland	Шотландия	[ʃɔt'landija]
Vatican	Ватикана	[vati'kana]
Liechtenstein	Лихтенщайн	['lihtɛnʃtajn]
Luxembourg	Люксембург	['lyksɛmburg]

Monaco	Монако	[mɔ'nakɔ]
Albania	Албания	[al'banija]
Bulgaria	България	[bɪl'garija]
Hungary	Унгария	[u'ŋgarija]
Latvia	Латвия	['latvija]

Lithuania	Литва	['litva]
Poland	Полша	['pɔlʃʌ]
Romania	Румъния	[ru'mɪnija]
Serbia	Сърбия	['sɪrbija]
Slovakia	Словакия	[slɔ'vakija]

Croatia	Хърватия	[hɪr'vatija]
Czech Republic	Чехия	['ʧəhija]
Estonia	Естония	[ɛs'tɔnija]
Bosnia and Herzegovina	Босна и Херцеговина	['bɔsna i hɛrtsə'gɔvina]
Macedonia (Republic of ~)	Македония	[makɛ'dɔnija]

Slovenia	Словения	[slɔ'vɛnija]
Montenegro	Черна гора	['ʧərna gɔ'ra]
Belarus	Беларус	[bɛla'rus]
Moldova, Moldavia	Молдова	[mɔl'dɔva]
Russia	Русия	[ru'sija]
Ukraine	Украйна	[uk'rajna]

20. Countries of the world. Part 2

Asia	Азия	['azija]
Vietnam	Виетнам	[viɛt'nam]
India	Индия	['indija]
Israel	Израел	[iz'raɛl]
China	Китай	[ki'taj]

Lebanon	Ливан	[li'van]
Mongolia	Монголия	[mɔ'ŋgɔlija]
Malaysia	Малайзия	[ma'lajzija]
Pakistan	Пакистан	[pakis'tan]

Saudi Arabia	Саудитска Арабия	[sau'diʦka a'rabijɑ]
Thailand	Тайланд	[taj'land]
Taiwan	Тайван	[taj'van]
Turkey	Турция	['turʦijɑ]
Japan	Япония	[jɑ'pɔnijɑ]
Afghanistan	Афганистан	[afganis'tan]
Bangladesh	Бангладеш	[baŋgla'dɛʃ]
Indonesia	Индонезия	[indɔ'nɛzijɑ]
Jordan	Йордания	[jor'danijɑ]
Iraq	Ирак	[i'rak]
Iran	Иран	[i'ran]
Cambodia	Камбоджа	[kam'bɔdʒa]
Kuwait	Кувейт	[ku'vɛjt]
Laos	Лаос	[la'ɔs]
Myanmar	Мянма	['mʲanma]
Nepal	Непал	[nɛ'pal]
United Arab Emirates	Обединени арабски емирства	[ɔbɛdi'nɛni a'rapski ɛ'mirstva]
Syria	Сирия	['sirijɑ]
Palestine	Палестинска автономия	[palɛs'tinska aftɔ'nomijɑ]
South Korea	Южна Корея	['juʒna kɔ'rɛjɑ]
North Korea	Северна Корея	['sɛvɛrna kɔ'rɛjɑ]
United States of America	Съединени американски щати	[sɪɛdi'nɛni amɛri'kanski ʃtati]
Canada	Канада	[ka'nada]
Mexico	Мексико	['mɛksikɔ]
Argentina	Аржентина	[arʒɛn'tina]
Brazil	Бразилия	[bra'zilijɑ]
Colombia	Колумбия	[kɔ'lumbijɑ]
Cuba	Куба	['kuba]
Chile	Чили	['ʧili]
Venezuela	Венецуела	[vɛnɛʦu'ɛla]
Ecuador	Еквадор	[ɛkva'dɔr]
The Bahamas	Бахамски острови	[ba'hamski 'ɔstrovi]
Panama	Панама	[pa'nama]
Egypt	Египет	[ɛ'gipɛt]
Morocco	Мароко	[ma'rɔkɔ]
Tunisia	Тунис	['tunis]
Kenya	Кения	['kɛnijɑ]
Libya	Либия	['libijɑ]
South Africa	Южноафриканска република	[juʒnɔafri'kanska rɛ'publika]
Australia	Австралия	[afst'ralijɑ]
New Zealand	Нова Зеландия	['nɔva zɛ'landijɑ]

21. Weather. Natural disasters

weather	**време** (c)	[v'rɛmɛ]
weather forecast	**прогноза** (ж) **за времето**	[prɔg'nɔza za v'rɛmɛtɔ]
temperature	**температура** (ж)	[tɛmpɛra'tura]
thermometer	**термометър** (м)	[tɛrmɔ'mɛtır]
barometer	**барометър** (м)	[barɔ'mɛtır]
sun	**слънце** (c)	[s'lıntsə]
to shine (vi)	**грея**	[g'rɛja]
sunny (day)	**слънчев**	[s'lıntʃev]
to come up (vi)	**изгрея**	[izg'rɛja]
to set (vi)	**заляза**	[za'ʎaza]
rain	**дъжд** (м)	[dıʒd]
it's raining	**вали дъжд**	[va'li dıʒt]
pouring rain	**пороен дъжд** (м)	[pɔ'rɔɛn dıʒd]
rain cloud	**голям облак** (м)	[gɔ'ʎam 'ɔblak]
puddle	**локва** (ж)	['lɔkva]
to get wet (in rain)	**намокря се**	[na'mɔkrʲa sɛ]
thunderstorm	**гръмотевична буря** (ж)	[grımɔ'tɛvitʃna 'burʲa]
lightning (~ strike)	**мълния** (ж)	['mılnija]
to flash (vi)	**блясвам**	[b'ʎasvam]
thunder	**гръм** (м)	[grım]
it's thundering	**гърми**	[gır'mi]
hail	**градушка** (ж)	[gra'duʃka]
it's hailing	**пада градушка**	['pada gra'duʃka]
heat (extreme ~)	**пек** (м)	[pɛk]
it's hot	**горещо**	[gɔ'rɛʃtɔ]
it's warm	**топло**	['tɔplɔ]
it's cold	**студено**	[stu'dɛnɔ]
fog (mist)	**мъгла** (ж)	[mıg'la]
foggy	**мъглив**	[mıg'lif]
cloud	**облак** (м)	['ɔblak]
cloudy (adj)	**облачен**	['ɔblatʃən]
humidity	**влажност** (ж)	[v'laʒnɔst]
snow	**сняг** (м)	[sɲag]
it's snowing	**вали сняг**	[va'li sɲag]
frost (severe ~, freezing cold)	**мраз** (м)	[mraz]
below zero (adv)	**под нулата**	[pɔt 'nulata]
hoarfrost	**скреж** (м)	[skrɛʒ]
bad weather	**лошо време** (c)	['lɔʃɔ v'rɛmɛ]
disaster	**катастрофа** (ж)	[katast'rɔfa]
flood, inundation	**наводнение** (c)	[navɔd'nɛniɛ]
avalanche	**лавина** (ж)	[la'vina]

earthquake	земетресение (с)	[zɛmɛtrɛ'sɛniɛ]
tremor, quake	трус (м)	[trus]
epicenter	епицентър (м)	[ɛpi'tsəntɪr]
eruption	изригване (с)	[iz'rigvanɛ]
lava	лава (ж)	['lava]

twister, tornado	торнадо (с)	[tɔr'nadɔ]
hurricane	ураган (м)	[ura'gan]
tsunami	цунами (с)	[tsu'nami]
cyclone	циклон (м)	[tsik'lɔn]

22. Animals. Part 1

| animal | животно (с) | [ʒi'vɔtnɔ] |
| predator | хищник (м) | ['hiʃtnik] |

tiger	тигър (м)	['tigɪr]
lion	лъв (м)	[lɪv]
wolf	вълк (м)	[vɪlk]
fox	лисица (ж)	[li'sitsa]
jaguar	ягуар (м)	[jɑgu'ar]

lynx	рис (ж)	[ris]
coyote	койот (м)	[kɔ'jot]
jackal	чакал (м)	[tʃa'kal]
hyena	хиена (ж)	[hi'ɛna]

squirrel	катерица (ж)	['katɛritsa]
hedgehog	таралеж (м)	[tara'lɛʒ]
rabbit	питомен заек (м)	['pitɔmɛn 'zaɛk]
raccoon	енот (м)	[ɛ'nɔt]

hamster	хамстер (м)	['hamstɛr]
mole	къртица (ж)	[kɪr'titsa]
mouse	мишка (ж)	['miʃka]
rat	плъх (м)	[plɪh]
bat	прилеп (м)	[p'rilɛp]

beaver	бобър (м)	['bɔbɪr]
horse	кон (м)	[kɔn]
deer	елен (м)	[ɛ'lɛn]
camel	камила (ж)	[ka'mila]
zebra	зебра (ж)	['zɛbra]

whale	кит (м)	[kit]
seal	тюлен (м)	[ty'lɛn]
walrus	морж (м)	[mɔrʒ]
dolphin	делфин (м)	[dɛl'fin]
bear	мечка (ж)	['mɛtʃka]
monkey	маймуна (ж)	[maj'muna]

elephant	слон (м)	[slɔn]
rhinoceros	носорог (м)	[nɔsɔ'rɔg]
giraffe	жираф (м)	[ʒi'raf]

hippopotamus	хипопотам (м)	[hipɔpɔ'tam]
kangaroo	кенгуру (с)	['kɛŋguru]
cat	котка (ж)	['kɔtka]

cow	крава (ж)	[k'rava]
bull	бик (м)	[bik]
sheep (ewe)	овца (ж)	[ɔv'ʦa]
goat	коза (ж)	[kɔ'za]

donkey	магаре (с)	[ma'garɛ]
pig, hog	свиня (ж)	[svi'ɲa]
hen (chicken)	кокошка (ж)	[kɔ'kɔʃka]
rooster	петел (м)	[pɛ'tɛl]

duck	патица (ж)	['patiʦa]
goose	гъсок (м)	[gɪ'sɔk]
turkey (hen)	пуйка (ж)	['pujka]
sheepdog	овчарско куче (с)	[ɔf'ʧarskɔ 'kutʃə]

23. Animals. Part 2

bird	птица (ж)	[p'tiʦa]
pigeon	гълъб (м)	['gɪlɪb]
sparrow	врабче (с)	[vrab'ʧə]
tit	синигер (м)	[sini'gɛr]
magpie	сврака (ж)	[sv'raka]

eagle	орел (м)	[ɔ'rɛl]
hawk	ястреб (м)	['jɑstrɛb]
falcon	сокол (м)	[sɔ'kɔl]

swan	лебед (м)	['lɛbɛd]
crane	жерав (м)	['ʒɛrav]
stork	щъркел (м)	[ʃ'tɪrkɛl]
parrot	папагал (м)	[papa'gal]
peacock	паун (м)	[pa'un]
ostrich	щраус (м)	[ʃt'raus]

heron	чапла (ж)	['ʧapla]
nightingale	славей (м)	[s'lavɛj]
swallow	лястовица (ж)	['ʎastovitʃa]
woodpecker	кълвач (м)	[kɪl'vaʧ]
cuckoo	кукувица (ж)	['kukuviʦa]
owl	сова (ж)	['sɔva]
penguin	пингвин (м)	[piŋg'vin]
tuna	риба тон (м)	['riba tɔn]

| trout | пъстърва (ж) | [pɪs'tɪrva] |
| eel | змиорка (ж) | [zmi'ɔrka] |

shark	акула (ж)	[a'kula]
crab	морски рак (м)	['mɔrski rak]
jellyfish	медуза (ж)	[mɛ'duza]
octopus	октопод (м)	[ɔktɔ'pɔd]

starfish	морска звезда (ж)	['mɔrska zvɛz'da]
sea urchin	морски таралеж (м)	['mɔrski tara'lɛʒ]
seahorse	морско конче (с)	['mɔrskɔ 'kɔntʃə]
shrimp	скарида (ж)	[ska'rida]

snake	змия (ж)	[zmi'jɑ]
viper	усойница (ж)	[u'sɔjnitsa]
lizard	гущер (м)	['guʃtɛr]
iguana	игуана (ж)	[igu'ana]
chameleon	хамелеон (м)	[hamɛlɛ'ɔn]
scorpion	скорпион (м)	[skɔrpi'ɔn]

turtle	костенурка (ж)	[kɔstɛ'nurka]
frog	жаба (ж)	['ʒaba]
crocodile	крокодил (м)	[krɔkɔ'dil]

insect, bug	насекомо (с)	[nasɛ'kɔmɔ]
butterfly	пеперуда (ж)	[pɛpɛ'ruda]
ant	мравка (ж)	[m'rafka]
fly	муха (ж)	[mu'ha]

mosquito	комар (м)	[kɔ'mar]
beetle	бръмбар (м)	[b'rɪmbar]
bee	пчела (ж)	[ptʃə'la]
spider	паяк (м)	['pajɑk]

24. Trees. Plants

tree	дърво (с)	[dɪr'vɔ]
birch	бреза (ж)	[brɛ'za]
oak	дъб (м)	[dɪb]
linden tree	липа (ж)	[li'pa]
aspen	трепетлика (ж)	[trɛpɛt'lika]

maple	клен (м)	[klɛn]
spruce	ела (ж)	[ɛ'la]
pine	бор (м)	[bɔr]
cedar	кедър (м)	['kɛdɪr]

poplar	топола (ж)	[tɔ'pɔla]
rowan	офика (ж)	[ɔ'fika]
beech	бук (м)	[buk]

elm	бряст (м)	[brʲast]
ash (tree)	ясен (м)	[ˈjɑsɛn]
chestnut	кестен (м)	[ˈkɛstɛn]
palm tree	палма (ж)	[ˈpalma]
bush	храст (м)	[hrast]

mushroom	гъба (ж)	[ˈgɪba]
poisonous mushroom	отровна гъба (ж)	[ɔtˈrɔvna ˈgɪba]
cep (Boletus edulis)	манатарка (ж)	[manaˈtarka]
russula	гълъбка (ж)	[ˈgɪlɪpka]
fly agaric	мухоморка (ж)	[muhɔˈmɔrka]
death cap	зелена мухоморка (ж)	[zɛˈlɛna muˈhɔmɔrka]

flower	цвете (с)	[ʦˈvɛtɛ]
bouquet (of flowers)	букет (м)	[buˈkɛt]
rose (flower)	роза (ж)	[ˈrɔza]
tulip	лале (с)	[laˈlɛ]
carnation	карамфил (м)	[karamˈfil]

camomile	лайка (ж)	[ˈlajka]
cactus	кактус (м)	[ˈkaktus]
lily of the valley	момина сълза (ж)	[ˈmɔmina sɪlˈza]
snowdrop	кокиче (с)	[kɔˈkiʧə]
water lily	водна лилия (ж)	[ˈvɔdna ˈlilija]

greenhouse (tropical ~)	оранжерия (ж)	[ɔranˈʒɛrija]
lawn	тревна площ (ж)	[tˈrɛvna plɔʃt]
flowerbed	цветна леха (ж)	[ʦˈvɛtna lɛˈha]

plant	растение (с)	[rasˈtɛniɛ]
grass	трева (ж)	[trɛˈva]
leaf	лист (м)	[list]
petal	венчелистче (с)	[vɛnʧəˈlisʧɛ]
stem	стъбло (с)	[stɪbˈlɔ]
young plant (shoot)	кълн (м)	[kɪln]

cereal crops	житни култури (ж мн)	[ˈʒitni kulˈturi]
wheat	пшеница (ж)	[pʃəˈniʦa]
rye	ръж (ж)	[rɪʒ]
oats	овес (м)	[ɔˈvɛs]

millet	просо (с)	[prɔˈsɔ]
barley	ечемик (м)	[ɛʧəˈmik]
corn	царевица (ж)	[ˈʦarɛviʦa]
rice	ориз (м)	[ɔˈriz]

25. Various useful words

| balance (of situation) | баланс (м) | [baˈlans] |
| base (basis) | база (ж) | [ˈbaza] |

| beginning | **начало** (с) | [na'tʃalɔ] |
| category | **категория** (ж) | [katɛ'gɔrijɑ] |

choice	**избор** (м)	['izbɔr]
coincidence	**съвпадение** (с)	[sɪfpa'dɛniɛ]
comparison	**сравнение** (с)	[srav'nɛniɛ]
degree (extent, amount)	**степен** (ж)	[s'tɛpɛn]

development	**развитие** (с)	[raz'vitiɛ]
difference	**различие** (с)	[raz'litʃiɛ]
effect (e.g., of drugs)	**ефект** (м)	[ɛ'fɛkt]
effort (exertion)	**усилие** (с)	[u'siliɛ]

element	**елемент** (м)	[ɛlɛ'mɛnt]
example (illustration)	**пример** (м)	[p'rimɛr]
fact	**факт** (м)	[fakt]
help	**помощ** (ж)	['pɔmɔʃt]

ideal	**идеал** (м)	[idɛ'al]
kind (sort, type)	**вид** (м)	[vid]
mistake, error	**грешка** (ж)	[g'rɛʃka]
moment	**момент** (м)	[mɔ'mɛnt]

obstacle	**пречка** (ж)	[p'rɛtʃka]
part (~ of sth)	**част** (ж)	[tʃast]
pause (break)	**пауза** (ж)	['pauza]
position	**позиция** (ж)	[pɔ'zitsijɑ]

problem	**проблем** (м)	[prɔb'lɛm]
process	**процес** (м)	[prɔ'tsəs]
progress	**прогрес** (м)	[prɔg'rɛs]
property (quality)	**свойство** (с)	[s'vɔjstvɔ]

reaction	**реакция** (ж)	[rɛ'aktsijɑ]
risk	**риск** (м)	[risk]
secret	**тайна** (ж)	['tajna]
series	**серия** (ж)	['sɛrijɑ]

shape (outer form)	**форма** (ж)	['fɔrma]
situation	**ситуация** (ж)	[situ'atsijɑ]
solution	**решение** (с)	[rɛ'ʃɛniɛ]
standard (adj)	**стандартен**	[stan'dartɛn]

stop (pause)	**почивка** (ж)	[pɔ'tʃifka]
style	**стил** (м)	[stil]
system	**система** (ж)	[sis'tɛma]
table (chart)	**таблица** (ж)	['tablitsa]
tempo, rate	**темпо** (с)	['tɛmpɔ]

| term (word, expression) | **термин** (м) | ['tɛrmin] |
| truth (e.g., moment of ~) | **истина** (ж) | ['istina] |

| turn (please wait your ~) | **ред** (м) | [rɛd] |
| urgent (adj) | **срочен** | [s'rɔtʃən] |

utility (usefulness)	**полза** (ж)	['pɔlza]
variant (alternative)	**вариант** (м)	[vari'ant]
way (means, method)	**начин** (м)	['natʃin]
zone	**зона** (ж)	['zɔna]

26. Modifiers. Adjectives. Part 1

additional (adj)	**допълнителен**	[dɔpɪl'nitɛlɛn]
ancient (~ civilization)	**древен**	[d'rɛvɛn]
artificial (adj)	**изкуствен**	[is'kustvɛn]
bad (adj)	**лош**	[lɔʃ]
beautiful (person)	**хубав**	['hubav]

big (in size)	**голям**	[gɔ'ʎam]
bitter (taste)	**горчив**	[gor'tʃiv]
blind (sightless)	**сляп**	[sʎap]
central (adj)	**централен**	[tsɛnt'ralɛn]

children's (adj)	**детски**	['dɛtski]
clandestine (secret)	**нелегален**	[nɛlɛ'galɛn]
clean (free from dirt)	**чист**	[tʃist]
clever (smart)	**умен**	['umɛn]
compatible (adj)	**съвместим**	[sɪvmɛs'tim]

contented (satisfied)	**доволен**	[dɔ'vɔlɛn]
dangerous (adj)	**опасен**	[ɔ'pasɛn]
dead (not alive)	**мъртъв**	['mɪrtɪv]
dense (fog, smoke)	**гъст**	[gɪst]
difficult (decision)	**труден**	[t'rudɛn]

dirty (not clean)	**мръсен**	[m'risɛn]
easy (not difficult)	**лесен**	['lɛsɛn]
empty (glass, room)	**празен**	[p'razɛn]
exact (amount)	**точен**	['tɔtʃən]
excellent (adj)	**отличен**	[ɔt'litʃən]

excessive (adj)	**прекален**	[prɛka'lɛn]
exterior (adj)	**външен**	['vɪnʃɛn]
fast (quick)	**бърз**	[bɪrz]
fertile (land, soil)	**плодороден**	[plɔdɔ'rɔdɛn]
fragile (china, glass)	**крехък**	[k'rɛhɪk]

free (at no cost)	**безплатен**	[bɛsp'latɛn]
fresh (~ water)	**сладък**	[s'ladɪk]
frozen (food)	**замразен**	[zamra'zɛn]
full (completely filled)	**пълен**	['pɪlɛn]
happy (adj)	**щастлив**	[ʃtast'liv]

hard (not soft)	твърд	[tvɪrd]
huge (adj)	огромен	[ɔg'rɔmɛn]
ill (sick, unwell)	болен	['bɔlɛn]
immobile (adj)	неподвижен	[nɛpɔd'viʒɛn]
important (adj)	важен	['vaʒɛn]
interior (adj)	вътрешен	['vɪtrɛʃɛn]
last (e.g., ~ week)	минал	['minal]
last (final)	последен	[pɔs'lɛdɛn]
left (e.g., ~ side)	ляв	[ʎav]
legal (legitimate)	законен	[za'kɔnɛn]
light (in weight)	лек	[lɛk]
liquid (fluid)	течен	['tɛtʃən]
long (e.g., ~ hair)	дълъг	['dɪlɪg]
loud (voice, etc.)	силен	['silɛn]
low (voice)	тих	[tih]

27. Modifiers. Adjectives. Part 2

main (principal)	главен	[g'lavɛn]
matt, matte	матов	['matɔv]
mysterious (adj)	загадъчен	[za'gadɪtʃən]
narrow (street, etc.)	тесен	['tɛsɛn]
native (~ country)	роден	['rɔdɛn]
negative (~ response)	отрицателен	[ɔtri'tsatɛlɛn]
new (adj)	нов	[nɔv]
next (e.g., ~ week)	следващ	[s'lɛdvaʃt]
normal (adj)	нормален	[nɔr'malɛn]
not difficult (adj)	лесен	['lɛsɛn]
obligatory (adj)	обезателен	[ɔbɛ'zatɛlɛn]
old (house)	стар	[star]
open (adj)	отворен	[ɔt'vɔrɛn]
opposite (adj)	противоположен	[prɔtivɔpɔ'lɔʒɛn]
ordinary (usual)	обикновен	[ɔbiknɔ'vɛn]
original (unusual)	оригинален	[ɔrigi'nalɛn]
personal (adj)	частен	['tʃastɛn]
polite (adj)	вежлив	[vɛʒ'liv]
poor (not rich)	беден	['bɛdɛn]
possible (adj)	възможен	[vɪz'mɔʒɛn]
principal (main)	основен	[ɔs'nɔvɛn]
probable (adj)	вероятен	[vɛrɔ'jatɛn]
prolonged (e.g., ~ applause)	продължителен	[prɔdɪ'ʒitɛlɛn]
public (open to all)	обществен	[ɔbʃ'tɛstvɛn]
rare (adj)	рядък	['rʲadɪk]

raw (uncooked)	суров	[su'rɔf]
right (not left)	десен	['dɛsɛn]
ripe (fruit)	зрял	[zrʲal]
risky (adj)	рискован	[ris'kɔvan]
sad (~ look)	печален	[pɛ'ʧalɛn]
second hand (adj)	употребяван	[upɔtrɛ'bʲavan]
shallow (water)	плитък	[p'litɪk]
sharp (blade, etc.)	остър	['ɔstɪr]
short (in length)	къс	[kɪs]
similar (adj)	приличащ	[pri'liʧaʃt]
small (in size)	малък	['malɪk]
smooth (surface)	гладък	[g'ladɪk]
soft (~ toys)	мек	[mɛk]
solid (~ wall)	стабилен	[sta'bilɛn]
sour (flavor, taste)	кисел	['kisel]
spacious (house, etc.)	просторен	[prɔs'tɔrɛn]
special (adj)	специален	[spɛʦi'alɛn]
straight (line, road)	прав	[prav]
strong (person)	силен	['silɛn]
stupid (foolish)	глупав	[g'lupav]
superb, perfect (adj)	превъзходен	[prɛvis'hɔdɛn]
sweet (sugary)	сладък	[s'ladɪk]
tan (adj)	почернял	[pɔʧer'ɲal]
tasty (delicious)	вкусен	[v'kusɛn]
unclear (adj)	неясен	[nɛ'jasen]

28. Verbs. Part 1

to accuse (vt)	обвинявам	[ɔbvi'ɲavam]
to agree (say yes)	съгласявам се	[sigla'sʲavam sɛ]
to announce (vt)	обявявам	[ɔbʲa'vʲavam]
to answer (vi, vt)	отговарям	[ɔtgɔ'varʲam]
to arrive (vi)	пристигам	[pris'tigam]
to ask (~ oneself)	питам	['pitam]
to be absent	отсъствам	[ɔ'ʦɪstvam]
to be afraid	страхувам се	[stra'huvam sɛ]
to be born	родя се	[rɔ'dʲa sɛ]
to be in a hurry	бързам	['bɪrzam]
to beat (to hit)	бия	['bija]
to begin (vt)	започвам	[za'pɔʧvam]
to believe (in God)	вярвам	['vʲarvam]
to belong to ...	принадлежа ...	[prinadlɛ'ʒa]
to break (split into pieces)	чупя	['ʧupʲa]

to build (vt)	строя	[strɔ'ja]
to buy (purchase)	купувам	[ku'puvam]
can (v aux)	мога	['mɔga]
can (v aux)	мога	['mɔga]
to cancel (call off)	отменя	[ɔtmɛ'ɲa]
to catch (vt)	ловя	[lɔ'vʲa]
to change (vt)	сменям	[s'mɛɲam]
to check (to examine)	проверявам	[prɔvɛ'rʲavam]
to choose (select)	избирам	[iz'biram]
to clean up (tidy)	подреждам	[pɔd'rɛʒdam]
to close (vt)	затварям	[zat'varʲam]
to compare (vt)	сравнявам	[srav'ɲavam]
to complain (vi, vt)	оплаквам се	[ɔp'lakvam sɛ]
to confirm (vt)	потвърдя	[pɔtvɪr'dʲa]
to congratulate (vt)	поздравявам	[pɔzdra'vʲavam]
to cook (dinner)	готвя	['gɔtvʲa]
to copy (vt)	копирам	[kɔ'piram]
to cost (vt)	струвам	[st'ruvam]
to count (add up)	броя	[brɔ'ja]
to count on ...	разчитам на ...	[ras'tʃitam na]
to create (vt)	създам	[sɪz'dam]
to cry (weep)	плача	[p'latʃa]
to dance (vi, vt)	танцувам	[tan'tsuvam]
to deceive (vi, vt)	лъжа	['lɪʒa]
to decide (~ to do sth)	решавам	[rɛ'ʃʌvam]
to delete (vt)	изтрия	[ist'rija]
to demand (request firmly)	изисквам	[i'ziskvam]
to deny (vt)	отричам	[ɔt'ritʃam]
to depend on ...	завися (от ...)	[za'visʲa ɔt]
to despise (vt)	презирам	[prɛ'ziram]
to die (vi)	умра	[um'ra]
to dig (vt)	ровя	['rɔvʲa]
to disappear (vi)	изчезна	[iz'tʃɛzna]
to discuss (vt)	обсъждам	[ɔb'sɪʒdam]
to disturb (vt)	безпокоя	[bɛspɔkɔ'ja]

29. Verbs. Part 2

to dive (vi)	гмуркам се	[g'murkam sɛ]
to divorce (vi)	развеждам се	[raz'vɛʒdam sɛ]
to do (vt)	правя	[p'ravʲa]
to doubt (have doubts)	съмнявам се	[sɪm'ɲavam sɛ]
to drink (vi, vt)	пия	['pija]
to drop (let fall)	изтървавам	[istɪr'vavam]

to dry (clothes, hair)	суша	[su'ʃʌ]
to eat (vi, vt)	ям	[jɑm]
to end (~ a relationship)	прекъсвам	[prɛ'kɪsvam]
to excuse (forgive)	извинявам	[izvi'ɲavam]
to exist (vi)	съществувам	[sɪʃtɛst'vuvam]
to expect (foresee)	предвиждам	[prɛd'viʒdam]
to explain (vt)	обяснявам	[obʲas'ɲavam]
to fall (vi)	падам	['padam]
to fight (street fight, etc.)	бия се	['bijɑ sɛ]
to find (vt)	намирам	[na'miram]
to finish (vt)	приключвам	[prik'lytʃvam]
to fly (vi)	летя	[lɛ'tʲa]
to forbid (vt)	забранявам	[zabra'ɲavam]
to forget (vi, vt)	забравям	[zab'ravʲam]
to forgive (vt)	прощавам	[proʃ'tavam]
to get tired	уморявам се	[umɔ'rʲavam sɛ]
to give (vt)	давам	['davam]
to go (on foot)	вървя	[vɪr'vʲa]
to hate (vt)	мразя	[m'razʲa]
to have (vt)	имам	['imam]
to have breakfast	закусвам	[za'kusvam]
to have dinner	вечерям	[vɛ'tʃərʲam]
to have lunch	обядвам	[o'bʲadvam]
to hear (vt)	чувам	['tʃuvam]
to help (vt)	помагам	[pɔ'magam]
to hide (vt)	крия	[k'rijɑ]
to hope (vi, vt)	надявам се	[na'dʲavam sɛ]
to hunt (vi, vt)	ловувам	[lɔ'vuvam]
to hurry (vi)	бързам	['bɪrzam]
to insist (vi, vt)	настоявам	[nastɔ'javam]
to insult (vt)	оскърбявам	[ɔskɪr'bʲavam]
to invite (vt)	каня	['kaɲa]
to joke (vi)	шегувам се	[ʃɛ'guvam sɛ]
to keep (vt)	съхранявам	[sɪhra'ɲavam]
to kill (vt)	убивам	[u'bivam]
to know (sb)	познавам	[pɔz'navam]
to know (sth)	знам	[znam]
to like (I like ...)	харесвам	[ha'rɛsvam]
to look at ...	гледам	[g'lɛdam]
to lose (umbrella, etc.)	губя	['gubʲa]
to love (sb)	обичам	[ɔ'bitʃam]
to make a mistake	греша	[grɛ'ʃʌ]
to meet (vi, vt)	срещам се	[s'rɛʃtam sɛ]
to miss (school, etc.)	пропускам	[prɔ'puskam]

30. Verbs. Part 3

to obey (vi, vt)	подчиня се	[pɔdtʃi'ɲa sɛ]
to open (vt)	отварям	[ɔt'varʲam]
to participate (vi)	участвам	[u'tʃastvam]
to pay (vi, vt)	плащам	[p'laʃtam]
to permit (vt)	разрешавам	[razrɛ'ʃʌvam]
to play (children)	играя	[ig'raja]
to pray (vi, vt)	моля се	['mɔʎa sɛ]
to promise (vt)	обещавам	[ɔbɛʃ'tavam]
to propose (vt)	предлагам	[prɛd'lagam]
to prove (vt)	доказвам	[dɔ'kazvam]
to read (vi, vt)	чета	[tʃə'tɪ]
to receive (vt)	получа	[pɔ'lutʃa]
to rent (sth from sb)	наемам	[na'ɛmam]
to repeat (say again)	повтарям	[pɔf'tarʲam]
to reserve, to book	резервирам	[rɛzɛr'viram]
to run (vi)	бягам	['bʲagam]
to save (rescue)	спасявам	[spa'sʲavam]
to say (~ thank you)	кажа	['kaʒa]
to see (vt)	виждам	['viʒdam]
to sell (vt)	продавам	[prɔ'davam]
to send (vt)	изпращам	[isp'raʃtam]
to shoot (vi)	стрелям	[st'rɛʎam]
to shout (vi)	викам	['vikam]
to show (vt)	показвам	[pɔ'kazvam]
to sign (document)	подписвам	[pɔt'pisvam]
to sing (vi)	пея	['pɛja]
to sit down (vi)	сядам	['sʲadam]
to smile (vi)	усмихвам се	[us'mihvam sɛ]
to speak (vi, vt)	говоря	[gɔ'vorʲa]
to steal (money, etc.)	крада	[kra'da]
to stop (please ~ calling me)	прекратявам	[prɛkra'tʲavam]
to study (vt)	изучавам	[izu'tʃavam]
to swim (vi)	плувам	[p'luvam]
to take (vt)	взимам	[v'zimam]
to talk to …	говоря с …	[gɔ'vorʲa s]
to tell (story, joke)	разказвам	[ras'kazvam]
to thank (vt)	благодаря	[blagɔda'rʲa]
to think (vi, vt)	мисля	['misʎa]
to translate (vt)	превеждам	[prɛ'vɛʒdam]
to trust (vt)	доверявам	[dɔvɛ'rʲavam]
to try (attempt)	опитвам се	[ɔ'pitvam sɛ]

to turn (e.g., ~ left)	завивам	[za'vivam]
to turn off	изключвам	[isk'lytʃvam]
to turn on	включвам	[vk'lytʃvam]
to understand (vt)	разбирам	[raz'biram]
to wait (vt)	чакам	['tʃakam]
to want (wish, desire)	искам	['iskam]
to work (vi)	работя	[ra'botʲa]
to write (vt)	пиша	['piʃʌ]

Printed in Great Britain
by Amazon